The Wallpaper Book

The Wallpaper Book

Geneviève Brunet

with 237 colour illustrations

Thames & Hudson

Contents

On the cover: (front) 'Lily of the Valley' by Sandberg; (back) 'Wallpaper Frocks' by Deborah Bowness.

Translated from the French *Papier peints, le langage des murs* by Ruth Sharman

First published in the United Kingdom in 2012 by
Thames & Hudson Ltd, 181A High Holborn, London WC1V 7QX

www.thamesandhudson.com

First published in 2012 in hardcover in the United States of America by
Thames & Hudson Inc., 500 Fifth Avenue, New York, New York 10110

thamesandhudsonusa.com

Original edition © 2010 Éditions de La Martinière, Paris
This edition © 2012 Thames & Hudson Ltd, London

British Library Cataloguing-in-Publication Data
A catalogue record for this book is available from the British Library

Library of Congress Catalog Card Number 2011935838

ISBN 978-0-500-51607-2

Printed in China

Introduction

Wallpaper may seem like a rather static subject, but nothing could be further from the truth. Its journey has been a long one – from the caravans travelling the Silk Road to the walls of today's designer hotels. It adorned the walls of palaces and grand houses before being embraced by the bourgeoisie and then by the working classes, and its colourful history is closely interwoven with social changes and historical events that have shaped the lives of many. A witness to the most intimate scenes of everyday life, wallpaper has always drawn its inspiration from its times, reflecting war and peace, revolutions and evolutions, fashions and customs, as faithfully as a history book.

Between its hour of glory in the 19th century and its fall from fashion in the 1980s, wallpaper found its way into every home and became a backdrop to many childhood memories. After some time in the wilderness, it is now back with a vengeance. The big manufacturers are digging deep into their archives to rediscover the best of their own heritage, while contemporary artists and designers are using this ephemeral but versatile medium as a blank page for creativity.

Wallpaper is perfectly in tune with our ambivalent age. Easily acquired and easily replaced, it suits our need for speed and changes to suit our whims. At the same time, however, it also answers our desire for reassurance, comfort and luxury. It straddles two very different domains – industry and artistry – and opens up and breaks down boundaries, blurring the line between art and design.

Wallpaper is constantly reinventing itself: it is an interior design adventure that keeps taking us down new and exciting pathways.

A Brief
of

History
Wallpaper

The story of wallpaper begins with the story of paper itself – invented in China and embraced by the Arabs, travelling with the trade caravans and dispatched in the holds of Portuguese galleons. And the story of paper is closely associated with the story of printing, which led paper on its extraordinary journey towards colour and design.

For several hundred years, wallpaper has been swept along by advances in manufacturing, powered by the Industrial Revolution, and now heading towards digital shores, following the currents of technology from textiles to paper, from craft to mass production.

Travelling from east to west, wallpaper has looped around the world, growing to popularity in Europe, then migrating across the oceans to America and beyond. It enchanted the aristocracy before being seized upon by the middle classes, adorning the walls of city homes and country kitchens. Over the centuries, it has travelled from Madame de Pompadour's boudoir to contemporary design studios, steering a skilful course between decorative art and great craftsmanship.

Wallpaper may be an ephemeral art form, but it continues to push the boundaries and explore new possibilities – and its journey is not yet over.

page 4: *'YSW Decenio' by Ybarra & Serret.*
page 5: *'Leaf' by Jocelyn Warner.*
page 6: *A selection of wallpapers by Clarke & Clarke.*
Previous pages: *Cloudy Mountains, an ink painting by Mi Youren, a Chinese artist of the 12th century.*
Opposite: *Chinese decorated paper, 18th century. The Chinese invented paper and adorned it with splendid handcrafted designs; they are therefore the originators of wallpaper as we know it.*

Treasures from China

From the Han Dynasty to Marco Polo

China was the birthplace of paper as we known it today. The recipe from which paper originated involved a mixture of mulberry bark, bamboo fibres, linen and hemp, simmered in a solution of wood ash, then beaten by hand. The man regarded as the 'father' of paper was an official at the Chinese Imperial Court by the name of Tsai Lun. Synthesizing the various experiments that had spanned three centuries during China's Middle Empire, in AD 105, Tsai Lun produced a system for manufacturing a paste which, when left to dry in a bamboo frame, resulted in a fine and even sheet of paper. For eight centuries, the Chinese guarded this process jealously, only allowing it to filter through to their Japanese neighbours. However, thanks to the Arab defeat of the Chinese at the Battle of Talas, in AD 751, Chinese prisoners of war were forced to give up the secret of papermaking and the Islamic world acquired a new way to record its religious, philosophical and scientific knowledge for posterity.

While western Europe was suffering from the onslaught of barbarian invasions, Turkey and the Arab world were enjoying the benefits of steady progress, and paper was carried by the caravans that travelled along the Silk Road that led from Persia to Syria and Egypt, where it replaced the more ancient papyrus. Its presence in Baghdad was first recorded in AD 793, and in Cairo in AD 900. The Moors took it to San Felipe in Spain in 1056, and to Fabiano in Italy in 1276. In the city of Fez, in Morocco, there were over four hundred paper mills in operation by 1184.

Paper arrived in France in 1348, before spreading to Nuremberg and northern Europe, and the first French mill was built at Troyes. From then on, the spread of papermaking was closely linked with that of printing, and by the beginning of the 15th century, paper was in common use.

It was in this period that the first decorative papers began to appear, inspired by the handpainted sheets that had begun to find their way back from China, via the Silk Road.

The wonders of Marco Polo

The first mention of Chinese printed paper appears to have been by Marco Polo, who was born in Venice in 1254 and is surely one of the most famous travellers associated with the Silk Road. Marco Polo explored the outermost limits of China's Middle Empire. He took twenty-four years to complete his travels, sixteen of which were spent in China in the service of Kublai Khan, notably in Yangzhou and Hangzhou, the largest cities in the world at the time. Back in Venice in 1295, he dictated an account of his travels in French, called Devisament dou monde ('Description of the World'), and better known in English as The Travels of Marco Polo. This lavishly detailed tale includes descriptions of Chinese interiors and of handprinted paper, mostly in the form of decorative panels representing flowers, birds and scenes from everyday life. Later, Dutch missionaries brought examples of these 'wonders' home with them, where they became a source of artistic inspiration throughout Europe.

The first wallpapers were decorative sheets brought back by merchants travelling the Silk Road; these became a major influence behind the fashion for chinoiserie in the 18th and 19th centuries.

Above: Paper by the great 18th-century Chinese artist Qian Xuan, Musée Guimet, Paris.

Opposite: Chinoiserie wallpaper, Esterhazy Palace, Fertöd, Hungary.

Early days

From Gutenberg to printed textiles

It was in the 15th century that the first 'domino' prints appeared in Europe – apparently originating in Germany, despite their Italian name. The arts of printing and engraving were in their infancy when these handprinted rectangles of paper first appeared, often bearing devotional or political images. The Arabs had been using paper since the 8th century as a means of disseminating ideas, and now printing made it easy to spread religious or didactic images among the masses in Europe. Gradually, people began pasting dominos on the walls of their homes, to conceal cracks or to decorate bedsides or overmantels. For the first time, paper was being stuck to a wall. In 1440, Johann Gutenberg revolutionized the art of printing and the end of the 15th century also saw the rise of woodblock printing. While the printing press made human knowledge widely accessible, it also encouraged the spread of more frivolous items. Dominos grew in popularity and became much more decorative in design, often embellished with little flowers or simple geometric motifs and peddled from town to town.

Dominos have their origins in the early days of printmaking. At first they were often used for religious images, but later became purely decorative.
Above: Domino printed by the workshop Les Associés, Musée des Arts Décoratifs, Paris.
Opposite: Domino with an image of St Nicholas, 15th century.

A brotherhood of domino-printers

During the 16th and 17th centuries, there were many makers of domino prints, known as *dominotiers*, who were united as a guild along with papermakers and playing card manufacturers. In Paris, their small workshops, which also printed almanacs and sheet music, were clustered in the Faubourg Saint-Jacques, a stone's throw from the university. Their stalls, huddled together on the pavements and under archways, gave off a pestilential stench of animal glue and charred bones. Other towns in France had their own communities of printmakers: these included Nantes, Rouen and Épinal, famed for its popular prints known as *images d'Épinal*, which were dominos under a different name.

During the 16th century, dominos decorated with coloured motifs were – in ninety-five per cent of cases – destined for use as bookbindings, linings for boxes and trunks, and coverings for screens. Occasionally they were also used on walls, as a discreet forerunner of wallpaper. At a time when most domestic interiors were dominated by dull shades, domino papers – manufactured in a range of sizes, known by names such as *coquille*, *carré* or *raisin* – offered a plethora of bright motifs in colours that included green, red, brown, yellow, blue and purple. The simplest were printed with repeat motifs from a single engraved block: chequerboards, squares, lozenges and circles were printed in black, then coloured using a stencil or a paintbrush.

The Papillon effect

During the Renaissance, aesthetic concerns had been restricted to the privileged upper classes, but by the 17th century, a new class of financiers and merchants were aspiring to live in beautiful surroundings too. The middle classes were unable to afford Flemish tapestries and Cordoban leather, which remained the preserve of the aristocracy, and so opted for paper imitations instead. Dominos appeared everywhere, adorning shops and the smaller rooms of great houses. They could imitate wood, panelling and marble, and the most luxurious of them used several printing blocks, producing interconnecting designs. Affixed to the wall, with overlapping seams, these gorgeous paper patterns were edged with specially designed borders or friezes with architectural motifs. In 1688, Jean Papillon, the first in a famous family of printmakers, began creating a more elegant version of the domino, called a *tapisserie de papier*; he laid out a motif of flowers and branches, then joined up the stems and leaves to create continuous panels. These wonderful designs ensured that flowers would be a favourite wallpaper motif for centuries to come.

SAINT NICOLA

A ÉPINAL CHEZ IEAN CHA·DIDIER Mᵈ· CARTIER D

A passion for printed paper

Philippe de Fabry, a curator at the Museum of Wallpaper in Rixheim, France, is an expert on the subject of dominos. For many years, he has combed the world, recording, classifying and filing these examples of the printmaker's art. If, by a stroke of good luck, an intact sheet happens to be found stuck to the back of a cupboard, it will be de Fabry who answers the call. He compares his job to exploring a dense rainforest, whose riches he discovers step by step, and every year he finds something new and unusual. He likes the idea that these sheets of paper preserve the memories — however modest — of popular imagery from a bygone era, the world of devotional images and playing cards. He also loves their texture, which he describes as 'pure chiffon', and in collecting these little works of art, bringing them together in one place, he is recreating a world where 'the notion of copyright did not exist', where workshops imitated one another freely, sending armies of merchants travelling across Europe, carrying with them these fragile leaves of paper decorated in bold colours, which still have the power to charm us today.

Above: Domino bearing the maker's name 'Aubert, Rue Saint-Jacques', c. 1750, Musée des Arts Décoratifs, Paris.
Opposite: *Domino printed in Augsburg, Musée des Arts Décoratifs, Paris. Both designs on these pages were blockprinted in black ink, and the colours filled in with a brush.*

Pictures for the people

'In Rouen, the printmakers who made mass-produced images were members of the guild of papermakers, cardmakers and printmakers, whose rules and regulations were drawn up in 1540 by the alderman Jean d'Estouteville... After taking an oath, a young workman was obliged to carry out a four-year apprenticeship before he could qualify... How did the printmakers produce those images that are so sought after today? They engraved their woodblocks — made of pear wood, which has a fine, close grain — using a tool that was extremely crude and simple... It was, of course, delicate work. They would make a number of broad incisions to indicate the general outlines and edges of the print. Then they would finish the work by adding crosshatched lines. If the printing was to be done in black, the block was nailed to the workshop table and a longhaired brush was used to coat it with black ink made from a mixture of lampblack and glue. The sheet of Auvergne paper, often slightly bluish in colour, was placed on top and the print was obtained by rubbing with a hard pad or frotton, made of horse hair and strong glue.'

Georges Dubosc, L'Imagerie populaire à Rouen, 1926

Above: *A flocking machine at work, from an engraving from* Grands hommes et grands faits de l'industrie, *France, c. 1880, private collection.*
Opposite: *The Louis XV bedchamber at the Château de Vaux-le-Vicomte, France. Flowers have always been a source of inspiration to wallpaper designers and this particular motif has been copied from a printed calico or indienne.*

Inspiration from the textile trade

The Silk and Spice Roads, controlled by the Venetians, facilitated free trade between east and west that continued unchecked until
Constantinople fell to the Turks in 1453. Then, for more than a century, Europe found itself cut off from the splendid goods that
it had formerly been able to import from distant lands. It was thanks to the heavy Portuguese galleons that sailed around the Cape
of Good Hope, a route opened up by Vasco da Gama, that the markets of the east were able to renew their trade with Europe, and
Lisbon became the leading port for silks and spices prior to the creation of the East India Company in 1599. Treasures imported from
the east included Chinese paper and handprinted cotton calicoes from India, adorned with flowers and leaves. The upper middle
classes fell in love with these fabrics, and the first textile firm to produce imitations of these **indienne** prints was set up in Marseille,
France, in 1648. After the revocation of the Edict of Nantes in 1685, however, the Huguenot craftsmen suddenly found themselves
deprived of the right to manufacture printed textiles and many of them emigrated, taking their expertise to England or Germany.
Those who remained in France began printing dominos instead, transposing their floral motifs onto paper. These motifs became a
classic element of wallpaper design, and came to replace the heavily patterned textiles that had previously adorned grand interiors.

The elegant 18th century

From Papillon to Réveillon

Although their names may not be widely remembered today, the history of wallpaper is indelibly linked with a handful of French pioneers, including Papillon, Réveillon, Dufour, Zuber and Leroy. It was their passion and dedication that pushed back the boundaries of wallpaper as a decorative art, allowing it to grow to a truly industrial scale but without ever losing its capacity for invention and innovation.

A master of illusions

During the first half of the 18th century, domino papers were still popular in France, although the market for them tended to be both urban and affluent. While a few artists were beginning to create reproduction paintings, the emphasis among contemporary manufacturers was on architectural pastiches. They even sold complete kits including colonnades, balusters, cornices, pilasters and statues, all reproduced in paper form. Meanwhile in Lyon, the French capital of silk, papermakers specialized in silk imitations. The Turkish embassy mission to Paris in 1721 boosted the popularity of Oriental-style motifs, extravagances that were a far cry from the more austere style of the *grand siècle*.

Jean Papillon's son, Jean-Baptiste Michel Papillon, began composing large-scale designs – later reproduced in Diderot and d'Alembert's *Encyclopedia* – inspired by the vogue for grand and exotic motifs, although he insisted on restricting himself to printing the papers in the narrow domino format and pasting them edge to edge to form the design – thereby running the risk of the occasional awkward misalignment.

Thinking bigger

In England, meanwhile, the most exquisite wallpaper was being designed. The technique of flocking was invented, using powdered wool fibres to give the design a velvety texture. The Blue Paper Warehouse opened in the City of London, named after its flocked papers that had a blue ground. Great names in English wallpaper manufacture included Thomas Bromwich, Isherwood & Bradley, John Baptist Jackson, the Eckhardt Brothers and John Sherringham, who was nicknamed the 'Wedgwood of Paperstainers'. In 1765, they had the innovative idea of sticking eighty sheets of white paper end to end to create seamed paper, which was sold in rolls, 12 yards (10.7 metres) long – twice the height of contemporary walls. These long and somewhat unwieldy strips – a format that

Wallpapers designed to fool the eye.
Opposite, above: *Paper fragments with an architectural design by Jean-Baptiste Michel Papillon (1723–40), Musée des Arts Décoratifs, Paris.*
Opposite, below: *Trompe l'oeil paper with a wooden panel effect.*
Left: *Screen covered with stencil-printed wallpaper in three colours, Jean-Baptiste Michel Papillon, c. 1750.*

has survived to this day – were laid on a printing table and, in a reversal of the domino technique, the inked block was then laid on top of the paper. It was a revolutionary idea, as was the introduction of distemper colour, the very matt type of pigment previously used only for stage scenery. French manufacturers of the same period were still using inks and oil paints.

Wallpaper's golden age

Jean-Baptiste Michel Papillon missed his chance to bring seamed paper to France. His father Jean had already invented an early version of it in 1688, but it was another manufacturer, Jean-Baptiste Réveillon, who adopted and set about developing the English techniques. It was not until 1753 that the fashion for flock wallpaper reached France. Madame de Pompadour made it fashionable, and château walls were henceforth stripped of

their tapestries and decorated instead with paper imitations that created the effect of damask, velvet and brocade in subtle floral designs. In 1758, the English writer and craftsman Robert Dossie described these paper imposters as perfect frauds.

In the later 18th century, wallpaper became a standard feature of everyday life, and Diderot and d'Alembert's *Encyclopedia* provides a detailed description of the manufacturing techniques that enabled it to become so widely available. Europe was enjoying a golden age. The Industrial Revolution was in full swing and society was increasingly being shaped by bourgeois values, giving rise to the enthusiastic consumption of manufactured goods. The thriving middle classes were not content to stare at plaster walls. Wallpaper arrived at just the right moment, and was able to imitate the tapestries, silks and wood panelling that remained the preserve of the most affluent.

Queens of style

Madame de Pompadour — the mistress of Louis XV — would nowadays be regarded as something of a fashionista. She was a patron of the arts and the epitome of the lavish refinement that characterized the art de vivre of the Enlightenment years. When the Duc de Mirepoix returned from his embassy mission to London in 1753 bringing high-quality English wallpapers with him, La Pompadour was quick to avail herself of this new luxury. At the time, wallpaper was widely used only among the petite bourgeoisie, but she promptly papered her dressing room, the corridors and a bathroom in the Hôtel d'Évreux (now the Élysée Palace). Other courtiers immediately followed her example, and wallpaper was suddenly all the rage.

Marie Antoinette also exerted a strong influence on contemporary style, and her refusal to be bound by convention gave rise to some eccentricities. Although her husband Louis XVI was a stickler for etiquette and tradition, she reacted against its excesses, papering the walls of the Petit Trianon and turning the boudoir into the most intimate of spaces. Thanks to Marie Antoinette's expensive whims, the Mobilier Royal purchased a great deal of wallpaper from the firms Réveillon and Arthur et Grenard, using it to adorn the courtiers' apartments and the ancillary areas at Versailles, and when the royal couple were exiled at the Tuileries for eighteen months in 1789, the walls were papered to create an instantly fresh look. Even the Temple was given a swift makeover with new wallpaper. The fact that his firm was granted the title of Manufacture Royale, however, did not prevent Jean-Jacques Arthur from becoming one of the bloodiest of the Revolution's sans culottes, while the Manufacture Réveillon was stormed by rioters.

Queen Marie Antoinette (portrayed here by Kirsten Dunst in the 2006 film Marie Antoinette, directed by Sofia Coppola) was a leader of fashion and helped to launch the vogue for wallpaper.

The great Réveillon

Jean-Baptiste Réveillon was the flagbearer of this golden age of wallpaper. When the Seven Years' War broke out in 1759 and disrupted trade with England, Réveillon used printing techniques imported from England and employed the very best artists, recognizing that success would depend on the subtlety and careful execution of his designs. From this point on, the craze for imitation fabrics and floral motifs grew – aided by the fact that, because it was now produced in rolls, wallpaper was no longer restricted to repeat patterns, but could be used to compose entire decorative panels.

One of Réveillon's designers, Jean-Baptiste Pillement, a painter at the Polish court, drew his inspiration from China and Turkey, or more precisely from a fanciful interpretation of those cultures. Working alongisde Prieur and the Italian Cietti, Pillement achieved wonderful colour effects. The motifs – chintz, rocaille and rococo – were no longer mere imitations, but developed a life of their own. In 1770, Réveillon's firm produced an imitation silk wallpaper in gorgeous shades, its pattern of flower posies tied with ribbons heralding the pastoral fantasies that came to be associated with Marie Antoinette. The excavation of Pompeii was just beginning and Réveillon had the idea of producing designs inspired by classical antiquity. His creations were soon sought after by wealthy Americans and, through his influence, French wallpaper became a fast-growing industry and found its way into respectable drawing rooms.

The firm of Arthur et Grenard were Réveillon's great rivals, but Réveillon led the way with his marketing strategies. His visitors – many of them ambassadors and royal heads of state – would be lavishly entertained at La Folie Titon, his grand premises that resembled Versailles on a more modest scale, and they would always be encouraged to place an order before they left. It was from the grounds of La Folie Titon that the first Montgolfier balloon took off – duly decorated with Réveillon designs. What better publicity could there be? At one end of the spectrum, Réveillon's sumptuous designs could require more than eighty printing blocks, but he also sold simple but charming single-colour patterns, and in ample quantities.

At the peak of production, there were some fifty wallpaper firms based in Paris's Faubourg Saint-Antoine, including Chauveau et Cie, Chapillon, Chapuy, Dubuisson and Arthur et Robert. There were also factories in Lyon, a city known for its printing: Simon, Desrieux Frères, Dusserre et Cie, Lecomte, Antonin Girard and Perrouillat, as well as Isnard and Schmitt, based in Alsace.

Many of these firms disappeared in the wake of the Revolution, changing hands as technology advanced and leaving behind a mere handful of treasures. It was in the area around the Faubourg Saint-Antoine that the Revolution erupted, and the Réveillon factory was pillaged and set on fire. Threatened by his workers, Réveillon took refuge in the Bastille and capitulated upon his return. On 14 May 1792, his associates Pierre Jacquemart and Eugène Bénard bought the business from him for five hundred thousand *livres*. At the time it employed three hundred workers and, thanks to Réveillon's business acumen and sheer daring, production had reached a quasi-industrial scale.

When wallpaper conquered the world

By the 1790s, there were some forty wallpaper firms in Paris, employing up to four hundred workers. Other firms were established in Lyon and Alsace. In Germany, the decorative arts were more focused on leather and tapestry, although there were a few paper manufacturers in Augsburg, working on a small scale. Wallpaper was often imported from France, where quality was higher; in 1797, Goethe stayed at the Gasthof zur Sonne in Heilbronn, and described its 'magnificent bedrooms, tastefully decorated with French paper'. It was not until the 19th century that the first big firms appeared in Berlin, Kassel, Potsdam and later Mannheim, many of them founded by former students of French manufacturers: Arnold, Behagel, and later Hochstaetter, Erismann and Engelhard. Some houses in the Hanover area are still adorned with embossed Lincrusta wallpaper, manufactured by Frederick Walton's company. One of the biggest German manufacturers today is the firm of Rasch, founded in 1863 in the town of Bramsche.

Switzerland, Belgium and the Netherlands eventually began to make their own wallpapers and were followed by Austria and later Poland. In Spain, the Real Fábrica de Papeles Pintados (Royal Wallpaper Factory) in Madrid was opened by a Frenchman, Giroud de Villette. Italy clung tenaciously to its preference for painted walls, but in Bassano and Bergamo, major centres for the manufacture of dominos and the home of the famous Remondini family, attempts were made to launch a fashion for wallpaper — some popular designs were even known as 'Bergamo papers' — but with little success. The US was the last to join the wallpaper bandwagon, in the mid-19th century, but rapidly compensated for the delay with their sheer quantity of output.

Even the French Revolution became a source of wallpaper motifs.
Above: Blue and gold design, decorated with fasces and rosettes.
Opposite: Design by Réveillon used to paper a room in the Duc de Mortemart's home in 1790. Both of these papers are conserved in the Musée Carnavalet, Paris.
Overleaf: Print depicting the looting of the Réveillon wallpaper factory on 28 April 1789, Musée Carnavalet, Paris. Réveillon's building, named La Folie Titon (on the site of what is now the Reuilly-Diderot barracks), was ransacked by rioters, assisted by workers from the Saint-Gobain factory: a foreshadowing of the storming of the Bastille.

Novelties from the 19th century

From Zuber to Leroy

When the Reign of Terror finally ended, Paris regained its status as the capital of luxury. France needed distractions as a way to forget the immediate past and the new Egyptian Revival style, inspired by Napoleon's expeditions to Egypt, found a ready market in affluent urban circles.

Blockprinting continued unrivalled for another couple of decades, but this method was superseded in 1830 by the arrival of new printing presses from England, huge machines built of cast iron. Until steam was harnessed for energy, the big printing cylinders were drawn by a team of horses that circled around the factory yard.

Thanks to the efforts of Napoleon III, however, a wind of change was blowing, and during the Second Empire, French society underwent more rapid changes than at any other period in its history. Paris and London now vied to become the cultural capital of Europe, and both cities hosted great exhibitions that provided a platform for the technical innovations of the age. Increased production coincided with huge social shifts, and the wallpaper industry underwent an unprecedented growth, blossoming into an art for all. Handmade products designed for an affluent urban market yielded to mass produced versions, and firms that had grown up in the heart of Paris began to move premises in order to accommodate enormous new printing presses. As France was undergoing this industrial and cultural revolution, Baron Haussmann was making his mark on Paris, replacing two hundred thousand homes deemed unfit for human habitation with the same number of new apartments that needed nothing more than a little decoration – with wallpaper, of course.

The reign of the machine

Two prominent figures are associated with technical advances in wallpaper production: Joseph Dufour, in Mâcon, and Jean Zuber, in Rixheim, Alsace, established their firms almost simultaneously, and, independently of one another, both invented panoramic papers in 1804.

These huge landscapes made up of multiple strips of paper were expensive handprinted pieces destined for the walls of wealthy homes. Most of all, however, they were good publicity for the companies who made them. The sublime panoramic papers that won prizes at the great exhibitions were the equivalent of haute couture in comparison to *prêt-à-porter*. Throughout the 19th century, they were the pearls of the wallpaper industry, and as machinery gradually replaced manual labour, these scenic papers were designed and displayed as a means of encouraging the less affluent to buy more accessible, mass-produced wallpapers from the same firms.

France's many colonial conquests overseas – Senegal, Cambodia, Cochin China and New Caledonia – were seen as demonstrations of the country's greatness and these distant lands provided the inspiration for a great many panoramas, which were viewed as both exotic and educational.

Sons of the Republic

The invention of continuous paper by Nicolas Robert in 1850 and the harnessing of steam power in 1860 eliminated some practical problems, speeded up the printing process and changed the wallpaper business for good. In Zuber's factory, for example, the number of colours that machines could print soon rose from twelve and sixteen to twenty-four and twenty-eight, and within one hour, some three hundred rolls of paper could be printed – a length of over three kilometres! New types of paper were regularly launched –

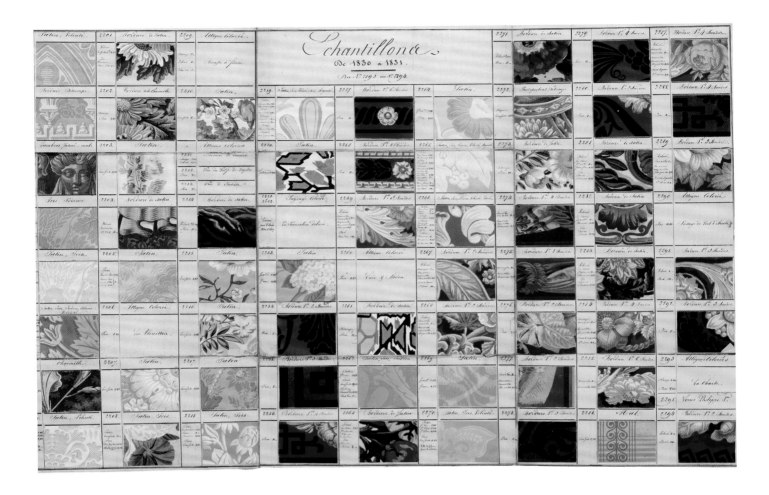

iridescent, embossed, imitation leather, imitation tile – as a means of boosting sales. By 1863, Paul Balin was advertising imitations of Cordoban leather, Genoese velvet and Gobelins tapestries of unprecedented quality. Other French wallpaper firms in the 19th century included Jules Desfossé, Tarquetil, Étienne Délicourt, Xavier Mader, Lapeyre et Cie, Drouard and – one of France's foremost manufacturers until 1982 – Leroy.

But machinery was expensive and in order to make it profitable, manufacturers had to find ways of selling their products to a wide audience. The price of a roll of wallpaper now became accessible to the average person on the street. In the 18th century, wallpaper had been the exclusive preserve of the aristocracy. Then the bourgeoisie got their hands on it and began purchasing from Jacquemart et Bénard, lining the walls of their townhouses with opulently patterned imitation drapery that fell in heavy folds around their windows. During the late 19th century, wallpaper finally found its way out of the urban centres and into the homes of the lower classes, as factories moved towards mass production and began making cheap goods of average quality.

The Leroy legacy

The water tower belonging to the Leroy wallpaper company still stands at a bend in the River Seine, at Saint-Fargeau-Ponthierry. The factory and housing estates alongside are a reminder of how, in the course of a hundred and forty years of history (1842–1982), Leroy rose to be one of the top wallpaper makers in Europe and an example of French industry at its most innovative. It was thanks to its founder Louis Isidore Leroy that wallpaper found its way into average homes and, along with Zuber and Essef, Leroy was one of the few 19th-century French wallpaper companies to continue operating well into the 20th century.

Above: *Travelling salesmen used sample sheets such as this one, printed by Dufour et Leroy, to display their wares. Musée des Arts Décoratifs, Paris.*
Opposite: *'Children with a Parrot' (c. 1824), made by Dufour et Leroy, Musée des Arts Décoratifs, Paris.*

Children at work

The wallpaper industry, like the textile industry, exploited children ruthlessly. They were obliged to work levers by climbing onto them and to crouch under the tables to operate the sieves that scattered wool fibres during the flocking process — all while breathing in lungfuls of the fine dust. It was the same story as in the mines: very few workers survived beyond the age of thirty. A law passed in 1844 and the arrival of mechanization fortunately released the youngest children from such employment, but the shift was slow to occur. In 1856, Victor Hugo was still denouncing child labour of this kind in Les Contemplations.

'*Our villa consisted of a wooden manor house with columns and two tiny outlying wings; in the wing to the left a tiny factory of cheap wall-papers was installed... More than once I went thither to watch how half a score of gaunt, dishevelled young fellows in dirty smocks and with tipsy faces were incessantly galloping about at the wooden levers which jammed down the square blocks of the press, and in that manner, by the weight of their puny bodies, printed the motley-hued patterns of the wallpapers. The wing on the right stood empty and was for rent.*'

Ivan Turgenev, First Love and Other Stories

America discovers wallpaper

In the early years of the 18th century, the former British colonies on America's east coast began to covet the touch of elegance that wallpaper could bring to a home. Lacking the expertise to manufacture it themselves, they imported it from England and later from France, after the Revolution. George Washington and Thomas Jefferson both indulged in the fashion for wallpaper, and were followed by the prominent families of New England; panoramas by Dufour and Zuber were particularly popular. When the United States finally began to produce its own wallpaper, it was on a typically large scale. In 1851, Jean Zuber, son of the firm's founder, wrote insightfully in the Revue Économique: *'North America is bringing up the rear in terms of wallpaper manufacture, but the young giant has entered the fray taking giant steps. Today there are first-class firms in terms of size and output. America has only been manufacturing for eight or ten years... but has gone straight for steam power.... This nation is not concerned about foreign competition, nor is it interested to know how things are done elsewhere. It needed a cheap product, one that it had produced for itself, and now it has produced it, on a massive scale. Although they buy luxury papers from France, Americans will continue to make their own paper for mass consumption.'*

Zuber: a panoramic pioneer

Rixheim in eastern France may not be the easiest place to find
on a map. However, this small town, close to the textile-
making centre of Mulhouse and to the German border,
became one of the focal points of the French wallpaper
industry in the 19th century, and production continues there
to this day. In 1791, Georges Dollfus, a manufacturer of
printed calicoes, started up a small wallpaper factory for his
son Nicolas — a natural enough step in a region dedicated to
textiles, since colour, pattern and blockprinting were central
to both trades. Georges Dollfus hired Jean Zuber, the son
of a clothmaker in Mulhouse, to work for the company as
a travelling salesman.

Nicolas Dollfus soon left, and Zuber became a partner
in the business six years later, when it changed hands and
relocated to the Commanderie in Rixheim, a former military
HQ. Then, in 1802, he found himself alone at the helm —
and about to embark on a long adventure.

The domino was still the popular format in France, but
things were about to change, and it was Zuber who would
lead the way in terms of innovation. He purchased a mill and
organized the necessary raw materials, and in 1829 developed
a system for manufacturing continuous paper — a transition
that was to revolutionize printing techniques.

Iridescence and ultramarine
Jean Zuber was a great inventor, constantly coming up
with new ideas, closeted in his ivory tower in Rixheim.

He blockprinted his first panorama in 1804; he invented
graduated colour, developed iridescent paper and patented
a flocking machine; he invented an embossing machine that
made paper look like leather; he pioneered the continuous
roll of paper, and invented a machine for producing stripes.
Working in his 'colour kitchen', the top chemists of the day
concocted the Zuber 'recipes', which remained a carefully
guarded secret. They also invented new colours, such as
Schweinfurt green and ultramarine. Bearing in mind that
a panorama could use as many as two hundred and fifty
shades, it is not hard to see that mixing them must have
involved a great deal of skill. Zuber himself recounted that
when 'Hindustan' was being manufactured, his colour mixer
was 'so worked up that within a few days he went mad'. Two
hundred years later, the colours still seem startlingly fresh.

Zuber was an exacting taskmaster, forbidding his
employees to speak while they were working and even planting
informers among them. By 1850 he had eighty blockprinting
tables operating simultaneously. The fame of Zuber wallpaper
soon spread beyond France's borders, its success due in part to
the high quality of the printing, but also to the quality of the
actual designs. Zuber recruited the best artists of the day and
gathered an exceptional collection of plants and flowers in his
garden and the grounds of the Commanderie, which served
as a constant source of inspiration. Freshness of line, realistic
design and naturalistic motifs were what distinguished Rixheim
wallpapers from their Parisian counterparts.

A machine like a man

The artists who worked for Zuber and his rival Dufour succeeded in creating a decorative style that has resisted the passage of time. Perhaps their creations owe their distinctiveness to the demanding natures of Dufour and Zuber themselves: Zuber was constantly intervening during the course of a piece of work, insisting that his workers make adjustments to a particular motif, shade or detail.

When the firm introduced its first steampowered six-cylinder machine, child labour finally became redundant. Manufacturing continued to keep pace with technical innovations under the watchful eye of a new generation of the Zuber family. By 1890, the new sixteen-colour machine was producing a quantity of wallpaper in a single day that a blockprinter working by hand would take four years to make.

During the 19th century, Zuber's firm acquired an international reputation and won prizes at major exhibitions, both in France and around the world. It was also the first French company to adopt mechanical printing and to import those huge gleaming presses that are now magnificently displayed in Rixheim's wallpaper museum.

'A rotary press, my little Frantz, rotary and dodecagonal, capable of printing a design in twelve to fifteen colours with a single turn of the wheel — red on pink, dark green on pale green, without the least running together or absorption, without a line overlapping its neighbour, without any danger of one shade destroying or overshadowing another. Do you understand that, little brother? A machine that is an artist like a man. It means a revolution in the wallpaper trade.'

Alphonse Daudet, *Froment and Risler*, 1874

Above: *The 'Views of Switzerland' series, handprinted from designs by the painter Pierre-Antoine Mongin in 1804, were Zuber's first panoramic wallpapers. The 19th-century manufacturers also referred to scenic wallpapers simply as 'landscapes'.*

The dawn of the modern age

From William Morris to Le Corbusier

Above: *A number of great artists tried their hand at wallpaper design. This three-panelled screen, now in the Musée d'Orsay, Paris, was designed by the couturier Paul Poiret.*
Opposite, background: *'Granville', a wallpaper design by William Morris, one of the great masters of the art.*
Opposite, inset: *Art Nouveau dining room designed by Charles Plumet and Tony Selmersheim.*

Mass production did nothing to promote the material or aesthetic qualities of wallpaper. Instead, cheaply produced paper designed for mass consumption tended to be mediocre, in terms of both paper quality and decorative interest; it was often thin and heavily patterned with motifs plagiarized from previous centuries, in dismal shades of brown, olive and grey. It was in reaction to this state of affairs that designers including William Morris and Hector Guimard formed opposition movements that paved the way for a new approach to the decorative arts.

Utopian dreams

William Morris, one of the greatest artists in the history of wallpaper, objected to the way that industry tended to focus on the notion of profit and the standardization of objects to the detriment of their aesthetic value. He longed to create a democratic Utopia where beauty and social justice went hand in hand. The effervescent Morris was

a textile designer, artist, writer, socialist and humanist, an idealist who inspired other artists, including the illustrator Walter Crane, to join forces with him in combatting the ugliness they perceived in bourgeois Victorian aesthetic values. Founded in 1861, Morris and Co., as his firm was later named, produced textiles, tapestries, stained glass and a host of wallpaper patterns, inspired by medieval art and floral and vegetal motifs. Underlying these creations were the principles of the Arts and Crafts movement: the conviction that all the arts are interconnected, and the advocacy of traditional craftsmanship as opposed to mechanization and industry. This approach was later continued by Art Nouveau, an idealistic movement associated with the rise of modernity, which was to catch the imagination of all of Europe. The Secession Style (Austria), Nieuwe Kunst (Belgium), the Stile Liberty (Italy), Jugendstil (Germany) and the École de Nancy (France) were all offshoots of this cultural phenomenon, and wallpaper was one of its major forms of expression.

Some of the most famous names in design were associated with wallpaper. In France, Émile Gallé and Louis Majorelle's organic forms, inspired by nature, are both sublime and startling, their abstract curves expressing an irrepressible lifeforce. In addition to designing a new silhouette for women's clothes, the couturier Paul Poiret produced several audacious wallpaper designs. Victor Horta and Henry van de Velde led the way in Belgium, while in Austria, Josef Hoffmann, Koloman Moser and Gustav Klimt formed the Vienna Secession, focusing on clean, simple lines.

The Art Nouveau style was as jubilant as it was short-lived – a firework of explosive line and colour that faded all too soon, its exuberant burst of creativity extinguished by the Great War.

The death of the motif

Art Nouveau was replaced by a style that was altogether more ornate. Reviving the flame that had been doused by the war, Art Deco derived its name from the International Exhibition of Modern Industrial and Decorative Arts, held in Paris in 1925. The Roaring Twenties brought with them a powerful wave of eccentric creativity, with

Extraordinary exhibitions

The Belle Époque had a keen sense of beauty, but a beauty associated with useful, everyday objects, such as those designed by Louis Comfort Tiffany, Émile Gallé and the École de Nancy. The motto was 'Art for all', and decorative art found its way into public buildings and even railway stations. These were the early days of photography and cinema. It was an age when bigger was better, when size and magnificence were what counted most — the fancy department stores, the Suez Canal, the Eiffel Tower and transatlantic liners. Paris's Universal Exhibition of 1900 was a realm of delights that captured the mood of the times, and it was here that Hector Guimard, the man responsible for designing the stations entrances for the Paris Metro, exhibited exquisitely coloured wallpapers that were the epitome of the Art Nouveau style.

Above: The Pavilion of Decorative Arts at the 1900 Universal Exhibition in Paris devoted considerable space to wallpapers. The panels on the rear wall of this room feature designs by Hector Guimard.
Opposite: A wallpaper in the so-called 'noodle style' of Art Nouveau forms the backdrop for this photograph, taken in Leipzig in 1904.
Overleaf (from left to right): 'The Day Lily' by Walter Crane (1845–1915); 'Leicester' by John Henry Dearle (1860–1932) for Morris and Co., 1911; 'Rushes and Irises' by Walter Crane; 'Bird and Pomegranate' by William Morris.

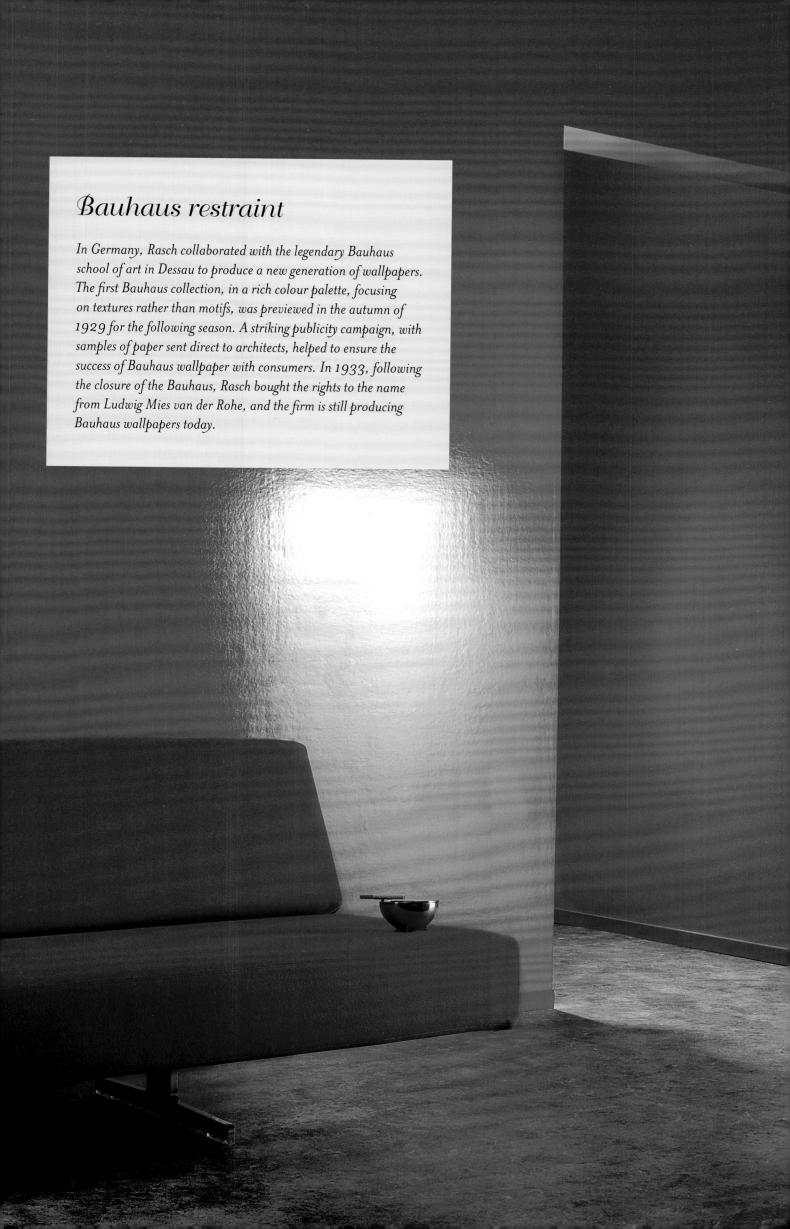

Bauhaus restraint

In Germany, Rasch collaborated with the legendary Bauhaus school of art in Dessau to produce a new generation of wallpapers. The first Bauhaus collection, in a rich colour palette, focusing on textures rather than motifs, was previewed in the autumn of 1929 for the following season. A striking publicity campaign, with samples of paper sent direct to architects, helped to ensure the success of Bauhaus wallpaper with consumers. In 1933, following the closure of the Bauhaus, Rasch bought the rights to the name from Ludwig Mies van der Rohe, and the firm is still producing Bauhaus wallpapers today.

Surrealism and Dada setting the tone. Automobiles and electrical appliances were the crowning glories of industry, and wallpapers by Pierre Chareau and Jean Lurçat reflected the vitality of the jazz age. The entire look of an interior became the domain of a new breed of artist, the interior designer.

In *Time Regained*, Marcel Proust comments ironically on the exuberance of some popular wallpaper, describing 'those modern decorations in which, against a silver background, all the apple trees in Normandy are outlined in the Japanese manner'. Proust had a point: those dynamic motifs with their strong, contrasting colours – explosions of red, pink and orange – were often Japanese-inspired. They were a last stand before the crisis of the 1929 stock market crash, which drew a darker veil over the cheerful excesses of the twenties.

The rise of social housing

During the period between the wars, wallpaper found its way into country interiors, and urban expansion also gave it new impetus. Social housing developed in Germany under the Weimar Republic, calling for simplicity and affordability, and by the end of the 1920s German manufacturers abandoned Art Deco for a more austere decorative style. Rasch turned for inspiration to the Bauhaus school, founded by architect Walter Gropius, and launched economical papers that were seamless and easy to use, their slightly embossed textures making them suitable for papering uneven surfaces. Friezes and borders were an anachronism within the limited spaces of new houses: fine stripes and imitation finishes became the functionalist response to urban growth, and millions of rolls of Bauhaus wallpaper found their way into homes.

In France, meanwhile, a new school of architecture, led by Le Corbusier, was promoting simple whitewashed walls. Nevertheless, the father of modern architecture designed two wallpaper collections for the Swiss firm Salubra (pages 74–75), in 1931 and 1959, describing them as 'oil paint in rolls'. Like the Bauhaus designs, they were imitation finishes, although with the innovation that the walls of a single room were meant to be papered in different colours. Le Corbusier never used them in his own buildings, however.

Left: *Bold and simple Bauhaus wallpapers are still produced by the German company Rasch.*

Motifs for the masses

From Lucienne Day to Andy Warhol

After the Second World War and the years of austerity that followed it, a wallpaper renaissance was slow to arrive. It was not until the 1960s and 1970s that wallpaper became truly democratic. The baby boom gave it a much needed boost, supported by a generation who were discovering the satisfaction of home improvements, coupled with the dizzy pleasures of consumerism. At the Festival of Britain in London in 1951, Lucienne Day's designs were a triumph for Cole & Son, while fairs in Stockholm in 1955 and Munich in 1960 also championed the cause of interior design. The wallpaper industry began finding ways to promote itself, while the first wallpaper exhibitions at major museums in Paris and Kassel gave it the seal of respectability.

During this period of rapid reconstruction, architects shrugged off modernist constraints and turned to wallpaper as an easy way of finishing off the new style of apartments with their smooth walls and limited floor space. The 'sex and drugs and rock and roll' culture permeated the aesthetics of wallpaper, often to spectacular effect. A wind of change was blowing and sweeping away the styles of a previous generation. Prized by trendsetters and ordinary folk alike, wallpaper became bold and modern. Its vivid colours and strong graphic motifs invaded every room from floor to ceiling, including the doors. Abstraction and psychedelic flowers became part of everyday life, and the influence of Pop art and Op art in the 1970s encouraged designs that were even more audacious. Andy Warhol, always in tune with the times, began to create wallpaper designs into his paintings, and a bevy of other artists followed suit. Outsize motifs and matching fabrics invaded lounge-diners and teenagers' bedrooms, raising the profile of these rooms within the context of the home.

Decor as we know it

It was technology that underpinned the wallpaper invasion: now that every household had its own kitchen and bathroom, there was a new demand for vinyl wallcoverings that were tough and washable, ready-pasted or even dry-strippable. Techniques such as flexography, photogravure

After the Second World War, wallpaper became a standard feature of everyday life, its cheery colours spilling into kitchens and lounge-diners.
Left: A scene from the movie Good Bye Lenin! shows a typical East German interior.
Opposite, above: 'Soil-proof' kitchen wallpaper by the US firm Glendura, 1956.
Opposite, below: 'Bistro' from the Palladio Wallpapers range, 1955.

Motifs that meant modernity

During the post-war decades, tastes in wallpaper varied from one country to another. The British continued to favour embossed papers, stripes and small classic motifs, whereas in Germany the fashion was for vinyl embossed papers. Dutch designs featured the country's traditional ceramics and windmills. In the US, garish florals ruled the roost and were often teamed with matching carpets — some hotels of the period still bear the scars. In France, Leroy was producing splashes of brilliant colour outlined in black, while Essef and Follot churned out florals and plaids.

Specially designed papers for children's rooms became fashionable, and the boom in social housing also created a surge of interest in wallpaper: no longer merely the expression of a decorative urge, it provided the means of putting a personal mark on an impersonal space, and repapering the walls became a ritual of moving house. Choosing a pattern was a way of combating greyness and uniformity, and stylized flowers or bold geometric shapes became a reflection of the modern world. Pop art and Op art styles mirrored the hippie vibe: 'peace and love' could be indulged inside a cocoon of orange, mauve and brown. And for the first time it was wallpaper that set the tone: everything else in a room — curtains, sofas, tablecloths — was designed to match it.

Above: *Mid-century styles – big patterns, bright colours and abstract graphics – even found their way into East Germany and are recreated in this room in OSTEL, an East German-themed hotel in Berlin.*

PHOTO CLAUDE ANGER

From boom to bust and back again

Until the 1980s, wallpaper was the most popular form of wall decoration in the West; but then came a complete slump and wallpaper experienced the worst crisis in its history. The pendulum had swung away from excessive colour and pattern towards simplicity and minimalism. Paint took over from paper, with austere white walls, sponge effects and plasterwork becoming de rigueur. The new interior designers had turned their backs on wallpaper.

The story was not over, however. The wallpaper tradition survived on a smaller scale, and beautiful, classical styles could still be obtained from upmarket firms. But in this age of design, the public followed the fashion-makers and despised wallpaper as fervently as they had once admired it.

But a dozen or so years later, the tables turned once again and wallpaper returned, rejuvenated in the hands of a new wave of designers. And so its story continues, as it provides a new source of inspiration for artists and the luxury industries, a vehicle for skilled craftsmanship and a vast playground for digital design.

and screenprinting provided the potential for all kinds of fancy designs. While it was now virtually indestructible, wallpaper became very versatile. It was ephemeral and therefore prolific, almost intoxicating in its quantity and variety. Quality, however, was slipping.

This fall in quality as a result of mass production soon brought a response, with new design inspiration coming from primarily from Sweden and the United States. Scandinavia – already a rich source of modern motifs during the 1930s – paved the way with the 'Good Design' movement, which was supported by manufacturers and designers and spawned a number of competitions that were open to artists. In Germany, manufacturers were quick to recognize the benefits of this kind of collaborative work: Marburg developed links with art schools and Rasch reissued its Bauhaus designs, as well as inviting some fifty artists to design collections. The motifs that resulted from these exchanges were contemporary and abstract, the forms more clear-cut and the colours sharper, reflecting general trends in architecture and the decorative arts.

It was through wallpaper that the world of contemporary design began to have an impact on the public at large. Women's magazines and 'homes and gardens' journals published in the post-war period helped to popularize interior design as a concept, promoting modern wallpaper styles and encouraging manufacturers to jump on the bandwagon.

Above: *An advertisement for Romanex textiles and wallpapers from the French magazine* Arts ménagers *(1953).*
Opposite, background: *'Toccata', a screenprinted design by Peter Shuttleworth for British firm Lightbown, Aspinall & Co. (1954).*
Opposite, inset: *Wallpaper was now manufactured on an industrial scale.*

Rooms with

a View

T

The earliest form of wallpaper was a continuous series of repeated, connected motifs, but this basic principle was completely overturned by the panorama, which consists of a single image and often tells a story in pictures, rather like a comic strip. This form of wallpaper dates back to the 19th century and is one of the most fascinating episodes in its history. Panoramas are works of art and were once produced only as one-off pieces, the equivalent of the Holy Grail to wallpaper collectors. But digital imaging has given this iconoclastic style of paper a new lease of life, providing designers with endless scope for experimentation: with a few simple clicks of a mouse, they can now decorate a wall with a widescreen image of a holiday snap, an enchanted forest, or a classical-style *trompe l'oeil*. Panoramic papers turn a wall into a blank page that allows the imagination to roam free.

Panoramic papers

The curved painted canvases known as 'panoramas' that excited so much public interest in the early 19th century inspired a number of attempts at large-scale wall decoration, but two names in particular – both keen entrepreneurs – are associated with the glorious peak period of panoramic wallpaper. Joseph Dufour produced his first grisaille 'English Garden' design in 1804, and in the same year, Jean Zuber created a series of 'Views of Switzerland' (pages 32–33) in colour. What was new about these gigantic panel-like decorations was that each strip of paper was different from the others: placed side by side, they created the illusion of a wall painting and, most importantly, they told a story. Scenes from classical antiquity, exotic landscapes, hunting scenes or battle scenes: these papers pushed back the limits of the physical wall. This was a century of explorations and technological conquests, a century of extraordinary adventures, and echoes of that vast world outside could now be brought within the intimate space of a domestic interior.

An unfolding story

Chinese paper brought back by the merchants of the East India Company may have provided the original inspiration for wallpaper, but now the panorama was fostering a growing interest in the Far East. Chinoiserie and other forms of Orientalism found their way into European culture, and major exhibitions soon began to introduce the landscapes and peoples of the Pacific, India and the Americas to a wider western audience. 'An important lesson about the world that helps to complete a child's education' was how Joseph Dufour described his designs. How many future sailors and adventurers daydreamed as children, gazing at these panoramas? Later, nature became the primary inspiration; a luxuriant natural world was brought inside townhouses and country châteaux, promoting the idea of an earthly paradise under mankind's control. Designed for large spaces, these landscapes always included a large expanse of sky and a dado of imitation panels.

In 1850, when a portrait painted by an artist cost a thousand gold francs, a wallpaper panorama could be bought for between sixty and two hundred. As time has passed, however, the skill of their creators and the precision of their execution have raised these magical decorations to the level of true art.

Above: *'Hindustan' (above) is one of Zuber's most famous panoramic papers, combining nature, exoticism and fantasy elements. It was designed in 1808 and is still manufactured today.*
Opposite: *Detail from a panoramic paper by Dufour et Leroy (1830–31), based on the tale of Armida and Rinaldo. Musée des Arts Décoratifs, Paris.*

A panoramic history

The term 'panorama' was first used by Irish-born painter Robert Barker, who produced a View of Edinburgh on the inside of a huge cylinder and exhibited it in the Scottish capital in 1787 and in London in 1788. With a little imagination, spectators standing in the middle of the room could feel that they were actually part of the scene itself. Barker's panorama was an instant success with the public and inspired a number of imitators, first in London and then across Europe and North America. The American Robert Fulton introduced the panorama to Paris and the artist Pierre Prévost began specializing in the new genre, exhibiting a series of panoramic works in a rotunda above a shopping arcade that became known as the Passage des Panoramas. These paintings included views of Toulon, London, Lyon and Antwerp, along with scenes from history such as the Battle of Wagram and the meeting between the French and Russian Emperors at Tilsitt. It was works such as these that inspired Dufour and Zuber to bring panoramas into people's homes.

The enthusiasm for the art form was so great that a bystander commented, in relation to the Exposition Universelle de Paris, in 1900:

'Do you like panoramas? They have put them everywhere… There is scarcely a section where one or more of these trompe l'oeil landscapes, panoramas or dioramas is not on display, and in the majority of pavilions, the tireless crowd push and jostle to get a better view of these pictures, which they seem to adore looking at.'

From Claude Lamboley, *Petite histoire des panoramas ou la fascination de l'illusion*, 2007

Forgotten luxuries

The French were the masters of panoramic paper. After seeing the success of panoramas at major exhibitions, companies such as Velay, Délicourt and Desfossé launched their own versions, and French scenic papers were exported all over the world. But barely fifty years later, these poetic masterpieces were almost forgotten, firstly because the arrival of mechanization and continuous paper led to the mass production of cheap wallpaper; and secondly because new houses were simply too small to accommodate them.

Panoramic paper experienced a revival in the US when Jackie Kennedy bought Zuber's 'Views of North America' (designed 1834) for the White House. Zuber then produced a collection of contemporary scenic papers, including designs by Jean-Michel Folon and Alain Le Foll. But this brief renewal of interest was on a very small scale, and panoramic papers remained a luxury item, the preserve of the privileged few. Collectors snap them up at auctions, and a few firms still produce these magical papers in the grand tradition, entirely by hand. These treasures can be seen in grand houses and luxury hotels such as the Hôtel George V (above) and the Hôtel Raphaël in Paris.

Above: *Classical-style panoramic paper can look completely at home in a modern interior. Here, a gorgeous grisaille design by Zuber adorns a room in the Hôtel George V, Paris.*
Opposite: *Zuber's 'Hindustan', in the drawing room of the Jardins Secrets hotel in Nîmes.*

Scenes from the space age

In 2003, the New York artist Adam Cvijanovic exhibited a panoramic tribute to Zuber at the Rhode Island School of Design Museum. Handprinted in forty-five different colours, **Space Park** *filled an entire wall and showed a crowd of spectators watching a space shuttle launch in Florida. While clearly contemporary, the subject matter also reflects tradition, in that it represents an episode in humanity's conquest of the world. The sky was an important element in 19th-century landscapes, and here a great expanse of sky surrounds the shuttle, while the palm trees mirror those in one of Zuber's most famous designs, 'Eldorado' (1848). A great trail of smoke connects the spacecraft to the earth, just as Cvijanovic links his work to that of the painters of the golden age of the panorama.* **Space Park** *is a splendid tribute to the genre.*

Modern murals

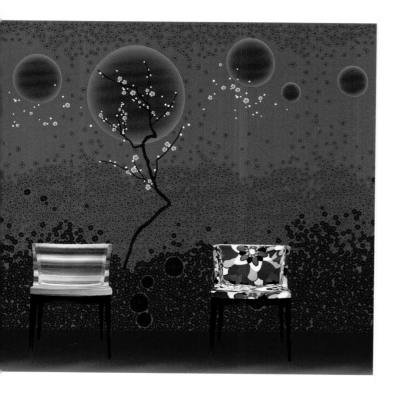

Today, scenic wallpaper is within reach of many more potential customers, thanks to the freedom of digital printing. These images may lack the charm of a traditionally made panorama, but they offer a new opportunity to travel while remaining within four walls. The magic of the colours combined with the power of the motifs makes it possible to give an interior a complete makeover that's both original and relatively inexpensive. The digital medium is interactive and dynamic, offering a range of expressive possibilities of undreamed-of richness and opening the way for boldness and creativity: the sole limits are those of the imagination itself. Yet, these modern panoramas are based on the same principles as their predecessors: they influence our perception of space by using strips of wallpaper that form decorative panels of various sizes, rather than a traditional repeat motif. The image disrupts the uniformity of the wall and opens up a new vista for imagination and creativity, creating fantasy landscapes that could not exist in any other form. Gigantic digital images can fill entire walls and even ceilings, and are longlasting too. And the job of hanging the paper takes half a day: you can push the furniture to one side in the morning and enjoy a new view the same evening.

Made-to-measure modernity

'Your walls have ears: tell them your ideas', declare the French company Conceptuwall (left and opposite, below), who are leading the scenic wallpaper renaissance by selling modern mural papers that can easily be used to create an amazing feature wall. Their range of designs – vintage wallpaper silhouettes against a boldly striped backdrop, fanciful garden scenes, a 17th-century *trompe l'oeil* room complete with fake panelling and empty picture frames, and stylized cityscapes – merge traditional motifs with a witty modern feel.

As well as a collection of designer panoramas, Streetwall also offers a made-to-measure service, turning photographs or artworks into unique mural papers, even in 3D, while MuZéo offers no fewer than 500,000 images on every possible theme, alongside a specialist picture research service. Paris Gang (opposite, above) have created a world that is both poetic and lavish, producing digital images on a variety of supports – non-woven, vinyl and flock. Overlap and transparency are used to create an interplay of spaces, allowing the graphic motif to become not just a decorative element but an integral part of an interior. The same company can also transform children's bedrooms by turning the walls into a series of storybook illustrations.

The Alyos Design range includes floral, minimalist and abstract motifs, along with *trompe l'oeil* pillars, and the firm can also produce custom papers based on clients' photographs. Also worthy of note are the German brands Extratapete (pages 58, 176–177) and Berlintapete, which specializes in designer pieces, as well as the Barcelona-based firm Coordonné, with its huge floral motifs that create a link between the natural and urban worlds. Since 1987, Plage has combined beautiful graphics with cutting-edge technology, producing the *Impulsions* collection, a series of limited-edition decorative panels, while Berlin-based Dr Nice offers scenic papers by artists such as Herta Müller, as well as bespoke pieces.

Above: *Digital printing offers huge potential for contemporary panoramic designs. This is 'Cerisier' ('Cherry Tree'), a mural paper by Conceptuwall.*
Opposite: *'Dyia' by Paris Gang (above) and 'Cabinet of Curiosities' by Conceptuwall (below).*

Back to the future

Artists and interior designers Dimonah and Mehmet Iksel first became involved with scenic wallpapers more than twenty years ago. Since those early handprinted designs made in India, Iksel creations (see above and below) have moved with the times, combining nostalgia with cutting-edge technology. In their Paris showroom, where magical gardens coexist with delicate wood carvings, a scanner designed by NASA reproduces the tiniest details of 18th-century motifs and sophisticated software scours historical documents in an attempt to give them new life. Their catalogue full of classical designs serves merely as a starting point: the rest depends on the miracle of digital imaging. The company works closely with many prominent decorative artists, all eager to share their ideas, and its creations can be found in a handful of luxury hotels, or tucked away in private homes. But for the Iksels, it is a matter of principle that their exquisite designs should be widely affordable. By producing a handful of the most beautiful motifs in a standard size, on non-woven supports in a fixed range of colours, they have made it possible for average people to treat themselves to a panorama or to splash out on a medallion, a chinoiserie design, a landscape or an Indian print — offering something midway between haute couture and mass production.

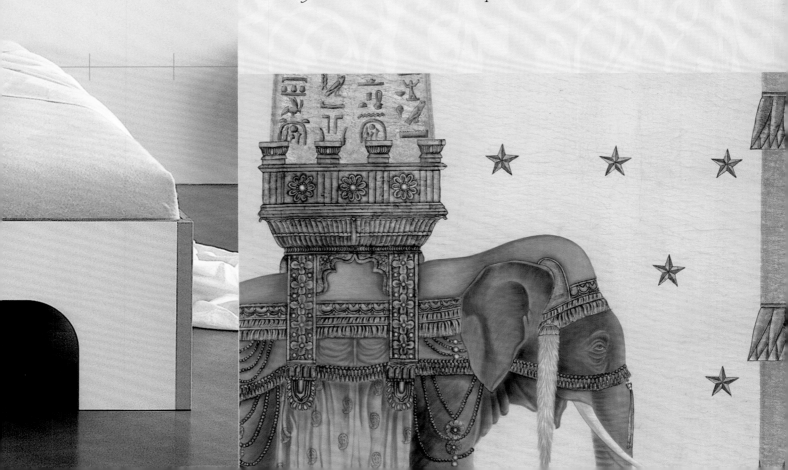

Previous pages, left:
*'Santa Maria' by Extratapete
lets voyagers travel without
leaving the room.*
Previous pages, right:
*Two designs by Iksel,
inspired by classical motifs.*
Left: *Two photographs by
Herbert Bayer, 'Self-Portrait
in Mirror' (1932) and 'Profil
en face' (1929), have
been turned into custom
mural papers by Spirale
Artisticker.*

A Paper

Paradise

Artists have always had a clear-cut relationship with wallpaper – either rejecting it outright or openly acknowledging its appeal, but rarely sitting on the fence. Aside from its perishable nature, the constraints of wallpaper as a medium are often a deciding factor: being forced to work within the restrictions of a strip of wallpaper and to integrate a repeat pattern can feel like a denial of artistic freedom, but it may also spur the imagination.

Of course, wallpaper rarely bears a signature to identify its designer. Major firms such as Réveillon, Dufour and Zuber enlisted the services of well-regarded decorative artists to exhibit their style and attract customers and impose their house style, but these contributions were predominantly anonymous. Some modernist manufacturers also collaborated with famous designers on a regular basis. At one time, the name of the artist sometimes appeared on the edge of the sheet, but the advent of seamless paper sounded the death knell for this practice.

This anonymity has contributed to the ambiguous status of wallpaper, which continues to be regarded by the general public as a relatively modest decorative item in comparison with other products of the applied arts, a distinction that is often undeserved.

Previous pages: *The 'Cestrefeld Wallpaper' (1895) by C. F. A. Voysey, Victoria and Albert Museum, London.*
Opposite: *'Woman with Daisy' (c. 1898–1900) by Alphonse Mucha, Wadsworth Atheneum Museum of Art, Connecticut.*

Art and craftsmanship

A surprising number of acclaimed artists and designers have created wallpaper designs, including Jean-Baptiste Pillement, Paul Cézanne, Henri Matisse, Charles Rennie Mackintosh, Josef Hoffmann, Alphonse Mucha, Salvador Dalí, René Magritte, Joan Miró, Le Corbusier, Frank Lloyd Wright, Niki de Saint-Phalle, Andy Warhol and Roy Lichtenstein. This fact serves to remind us that links between the arts have always existed, and that great artists have never been afraid of treating wallpaper as a creative medium. Although these experiments were frequently one-offs and often very discreet, some dazzling creations have resulted from them. After delving a little deeper into the history of wallpaper, we would have to be very mean-spirited indeed to regard it as merely a minor decorative art.

Anonymous artists

Albrecht Dürer seems to have been the first artist to become involved with wallpaper. A repeat pattern featured in one of his small woodcuts was used to create a decor celebrating the marriage of two of Emperor Maximilian's grandchildren in Vienna, in 1515; this became the first wallpaper designed by a great master. Dürer went on to produce other printed motifs, but he was an exception. During the 16th and 17th centuries, European draughtsmen simply treated wallpaper in the same way as tapestry, using rapidly drawn figurative motifs. Not until the 18th century did the Englishman John Baptist Jackson, a pupil of Papillon, rework motifs by Nicolas Poussin, Claude Lorrain and Paolo Veronese in his delicate papers.

Above: Thirty Years or La Vie en Rose (1931) by Raoul Dufy. Musée d'Art Moderne de la Ville de Paris. **Opposite:** 'Golden Lily' by John Henry Dearle, produced by Morris and Co. Victoria & Albert Museum, London.

Intricate mysteries

'I think the real way to deal successfully with designing for paper-hangings is to accept their mechanical nature frankly, to avoid falling into the trap of trying to make your paper look as if it were painted by hand. Here is the place, if anywhere, for dots and lines and hatchings: mechanical enrichment is of the first necessity in it. After that you may be as intricate and elaborate in your pattern as you please; nay, the more and the more mysteriously you interweave your sprays and stems the better for your purpose, as the whole thing has to be pasted flat on a wall, and the cost of all this intricacy will but come out of your own brain and hand.'

William Morris, *The Lesser Arts of Life*, 1882

In the 19th century, the vogue for panoramic paper encouraged painters to work for the major manufacturers, but their identities remained unknown. If we read the lengthy and often heated correspondence that passed between Jean Zuber and his artists, it becomes clear that every one of his designs was a major artistic challenge. Shut away in secret, the artists who worked for Pillement, Lavallée-Poussin, Prieur and the Gobelins workshops were denied any credit for their wallpaper designs, despite their reputations in the fields of paintings, textiles or ceramics. It was not until the 1855 International Exhibition in Paris that Jules Desfossé allowed Thomas Couture's signature to appear on the panorama 'Les Prodigues' (see above). This was a first step in the reconciliation of wallpaper and art.

The turn of the century

At the end of the 19th century, a buoyant spirit of optimism prevailed with regard to progress and human potential, and artists were keen to cross the boundaries between the fine arts and the decorative arts. However, mechanization, a product of the industrial era, had already begun to create a huge gulf between these two poles of artistic production. Following in the wake of the prolific William Morris and his disciples in the Arts and Crafts movement, who sought to establish a perfect harmony between architecture, furnishings and decoration, a host of artists put their names to some incredible designs.

The Belgians Henry van de Velde and Victor Horta laid the foundations for Art Nouveau with their wallpaper designs; both of them gave up painting to devote themselves to the decorative arts. The voluptuous curves drawn by Hector Guimard (page 36), Alphonse Mucha (page 65) and Otto Eckmann, the sparse and structured forms of Charles Rennie Mackintosh, Josef Hoffmann, Koloman Moser and Otto Wagner, and Gustav Klimt's flat decorative expanses: all of these had a huge influence on turn-of-the-century interiors.

The Art Deco movement was a further demonstration of the fact that all forms of artistic expression are interconnected: the painter and printmaker Marie Laurencin, the cabinetmaker (and son of a wallpaper manufacturer) Paul Follot, and the furniture designer and interior designer Jacques-Émile Ruhlmann are just some of the names who designed wallpapers in this period. The couturier Paul Poiret, encouraged by his friend Raoul Dufy, also produced several designs for wallcoverings. In the 1930s, tapestry artist Jean Lurçat enthusiastically embraced the decorative arts at the same time as his friend Pablo Picasso, and designed some wallpapers with a strong Dada influence.

This prolific period was to be the last in which high-quality wallpaper designs by artists were still produced by craftsmen according to traditional methods, working in limited print runs and sometimes even using blockprinting.

'A constant reminder'

'We would have supper with Derain, the famous painter, who was a cyclist, and in the midst of a life full of dreariness and hardship, it was some consolation that we were able to make a few feeble gestures in the direction of the arts, which was our favourite subject. We were living in an old lodging house called the Hôtel du Maure, where the only way for me to have a clean room was to repaper it. I put up a tricolour paper, which was a constant reminder of why I was there. I have heard that the owner of the place is still showing the room today as if it had belonged to Bonaparte himself... It was in this memorable setting that Derain began my portrait.'

Paul Poiret, describing a stay in Lisieux in 1914, in *En habillant l'époque*, 1930

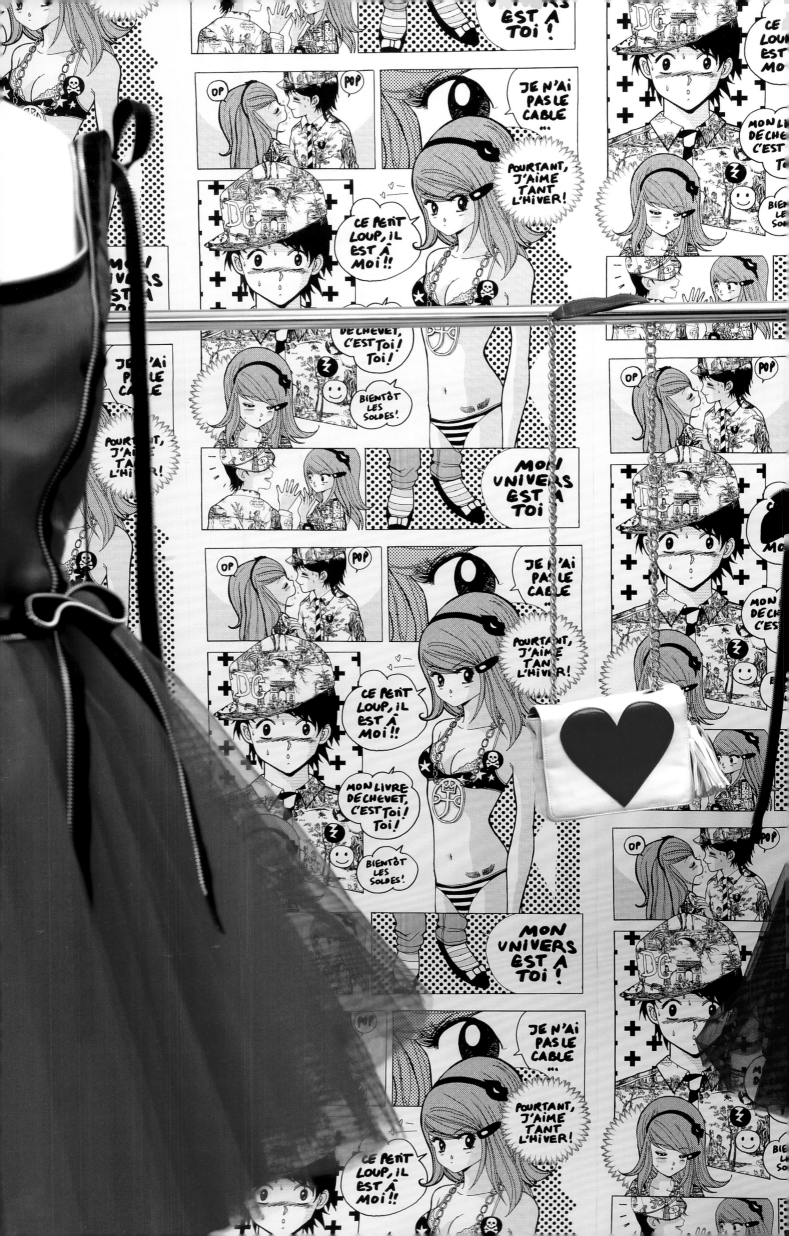

Fashion and wallpaper

Paul Poiret, the great couturier of the 1920s, was the first fashion designer to turn his hand to wallpaper. Poiret was well regarded in artistic circles and had a good eye for interior design, and in 1912 he founded his own design school, the Atelier Martine, which produced a great many wallpaper designs that were distinguished by their brilliant colour palette and bold compositions. Some 21st-century fashionistas have followed his lead and now treat wallpaper as another medium for expressing their ideas. The wallcoverings designed by the whimsical and multifaceted Jean-Charles de Castelbajac (see left and pages 112–113), for example, are nothing if not vibrant, and the famously daring Vivienne Westwood has created a magnificent collection for Cole & Son (see above and page 133). Vincent Darré has also ventured into the world of wallpaper (page 215), while Martin Margiela, fashion's man of mystery, emerged from the shadows with the creation of a set of wallpaper designs reflecting his elegant brand and inspired by the decor of his former Paris headquarters (pages 216–217).

Left: *A manga-inspired design by Jean-Charles de Castelbajac, one of a collection for the French firm Lutèce.*
Above: *'Squiggle' by legendary British fashion designer Vivienne Westwood, part of a collection for Cole & Son.*

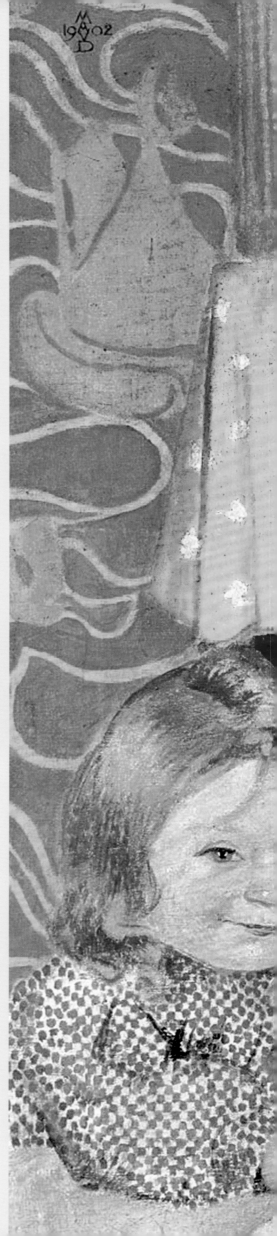

At home with the Nabis

The group of painters known as the Nabis did a great deal to promote the relationship between fine art and the decorative arts at the end of the 19th century, regarding the latter as a natural extension of their own artistic methods. The desire to make art an integral part of everyday life was one of their fundamental principles and led Maurice Denis, Paul Ranson and their colleagues to design and exhibit wallpaper motifs. These wallpapers sometimes appear in the backgrounds of their paintings, as a demonstration of their own beliefs in action.

The painters of the Nabi group designed wallpapers that also feature prominently in their paintings.
Above: Portrait of Eva Meurier in Green Dress *(1891) by Maurice Denis. Private collection.*
Opposite: Family Portrait in Blue and Yellow *(1902) by Maurice Denis, featuring 'Les Bateaux roses' wallpaper in the background. Private collection.*

Merging form and functionalism

As wallpaper production developed into a full-scale industry, manufacturers decided to revive the idea of collaborating with artists and designers, in the hope that this association would give their products both artistic legitimacy and greater publicity – a marketing strategy that is still very much in operation today.

From the Bauhaus to Le Corbusier

By 1929, Art Deco was no longer an accurate reflection of the austere mood of the times, and the German firm Rasch looked instead towards the designers of the Bauhaus school. The aim of the Bauhaus was to bring together the fine arts and the applied arts under one umbrella, and its wallpapers (pages 40–41) – although of rather limited artistic interest – were a commercial success.

During the same period, Swiss architect Le Corbusier, an arch-opponent of all things elaborate, was campaigning for pared-down simplicity and purity. Le Corbusier, who always included furniture and wall finishes in his designs, was renowned for mounting a crusade against the decorative arts in his journal *L'Esprit nouveau* and came up with the so-called *loi de Ripolin* or 'whitewash law', which stated: 'Every citizen is required to replace his hangings, his damasks, his wallpapers, his stencils, with a plain coat of whitewash.' It may have been something of a contradiction, therefore, when, in 1931 and again in 1959, he collaborated with the Swiss firm Salubra on two wallpaper collections (above right). However, these were all either plain or decorated with dots or simple geometric motifs, so as not to interfere with the architecture.

Above right: *In their 1959 catalogue, the Swiss firm Salubra included a range of wallpapers designed by Le Corbusier.*
Below right: *A Bauhaus wallpaper reissued by the German firm Rasch (2009), together with the famous chaise longue designed by Le Corbusier, Pierre Jeanneret and Charlotte Perriand.*

Le Corbusier in colour

Le Corbusier's wallpaper designs reflected his enormous experience as a painter and an architect. He described his wallpaper as 'oil paint in rolls' and selected forty-three colours for his first range in 1931, as well as inventing innovative 'colour keyboards' that allowed the colour samples to be mixed and matched as appropriate. Le Corbusier mostly restricted his personal use of his wallpaper to his collages, however, perhaps anxious that he had 'set the gate of the garden of temptation ajar'. His second collection for Salubra, in 1959, used twenty strong colours, bringing traditional wallpaper up to date by reconciling it with an avant-garde 20th-century approach.

Specialists in style

The craze for wallpaper at the end of the Second World War and the frenzy of reconstruction and consumerism that followed once again encouraged manufacturers to involve artists in designing the key elements of their collections. Rasch reissued its Bauhaus wallpapers and invited some fifty artists, including textile designers Margret Hildebrand and Lucienne Day, and the Junger Westen artists' group, to produce designs. Published in 1939 under the auspices of Josef Hoffmann, one of the founders of the Vienna Secession, Rasch's *Wiener Künstlertapeten* ('Viennese artists' wallpapers') collection was fantastically elegant, while Marburg's *Neue Form* range, designed by Elsbeth Kupferoth, was widely imitated.

In the US, Katzenbach & Warren enlisted the services of Henri Matisse, Joan Miró, Alexander Calder and Roberto Matta for its *Mural Scroll* collection in 1948, while Schiffer Prints, a New York company, commissioned designs from George Nelson and Ray Eames.

Abstraction and architecture

This was the era of abstraction and figurative designs, with wallpapers by Charles Portel, René Crevel (pages 202–203), Suzanne Fourcade and later Paule Marrot and Suzanne Fontan, whose designs combined 18th-century influences with a real lightness of touch. Polish-born Zofia Rostad – another *grande dame* of wallpaper design – trained under Paule Marrot and was influenced by Victor Vasarely, Pierre Soulages, Hans Hartung and Sonia Delaunay. The first designer to have her own signature collection produced by Essef

(the firm that also published Léonor Fini's 'Lendemain de fête' wallpaper), Rostad designed for a wide audience, as did Denise Fayolle, designer for the French chainstore Prisunic, who revolutionized the aesthetics of mass production during the 1960s.

Twenty years after Le Corbusier had designed his 'oil paint in rolls', Frank Lloyd Wright brought wallpapers and his architectural work together by designing a range of coordinating papers and fabrics for US company Schumacher, named the *Taliesin Line*.

Brief encounters

For some artists, wallpaper design was simply a means of earning a living. In his book *Le Monde du surréalisme*, Gérard de Cortanze tells us that René Magritte was 'forced to design little bunches of cabbage roses in a wallpaper factory in order to survive'. For others, wallpaper was merely a brief encounter, as in the case of Salvador Dalí, who produced a single design for Rasch, entitled 'Cervantes' (see right), although it was a bestseller. Another one-hit wonder was Belgian artist and illustrator Jean-Michel Folon, who incorporated his signature flying birdmen into a design entitled 'Foultitude', published by Zuber in 1969.

A number of modernist artists designed wallpapers, among them Salvador Dalí, Henri Matisse, Joan Miró, Alexander Calder, Roberto Matta, René Magritte and Jean-Michel Folon. Here, we see Dalí's bestselling design 'Cervantes' (1960), for the German firm Rasch.

Art on the Wall

Although many artists have been happy to transpose their work onto wallpaper, it was a long time before wallpaper found its way into art, maybe because artists were worried that the motifs might dominate their canvases. At any rate, it was not until the advent of realism in the 19th century that wallpaper was depicted in the background of paintings – in the works of artists such as Cézanne and and the Nabis, who painted it enthusiastically. Later artists, from Andy Warhol onwards, have adopted a very different approach, ignoring all the rules and using wallpaper entirely for their own purposes, as a medium on which to project their imaginations or make a political statement, tackling the basic notion of what wallpaper is and what it is for.

Right: After the Bath
(1889) by Edgar Degas,
State Hermitage Museum,
St Petersburg.
Opposite: La Toilette
(c. 1908) by Pierre Bonnard,
Musée d'Orsay, Paris.
Both artists depicted
wallpaper in their paintings.
Previous pages: 'Cow'
(1971), a wallpaper design
by Andy Warhol, Whitney
Museum of American Art,
New York.

Encounters on canvas

The painter Adolphe Monticelli – acknowledged as a source of inspiration by Van Gogh – incorporated pieces of wallpaper into his paintings, just as the Cubists were later to do in their collages; but it was Cézanne who first depicted wallpaper in situ, and in fact it features significantly in twenty-five of his canvases. Pissarro was a close friend of Cézanne's for twenty years and shared many of his artistic experiments, and he adopted the same practice. Edgar Degas portrayed *The Bellelli Family* in front of a floral wallpaper and the walls in *Interior (The Rape)* are similarly adorned. When Renoir painted his *Portrait of Julie Manet*, it was in front of a wallpaper backdrop, and although Manet's scandalous *Olympia* attracts far more attention that the wallpaper behind her, it is present in the scene nonetheless.

Intimate scenes in the work of the Nabis

The Nabis and the post-Impressionists, including Pierre Bonnard, Édouard Vuillard and Félix Vallotton, specialized in painting quiet, intimate scenes that glorified everyday life, using wallpaper as a backdrop for their tender family portraits and moving nude studies. Vuillard was a master in this field and in some of his domestic interiors the figures seem almost to be part of the walls themselves. Wallpaper could also serve as a means of underlining the simplicity of an interior. In *Annette's Soup*, the woman's dress blends with the wallpaper's colourful pattern, which in turn evokes the floral tapestries of the late Middle Ages, while the triptych *Interior with Pink Wallpaper* is conceived as a kind of hymn to the decorative arts.

Maurice Denis produced a number of designs for the wallpaper industry, and wallpaper also featured extensively in his paintings – amusingly enough, his own design 'Les Bateaux roses' appears as a backdrop in his *Family Portrait in Blue and Yellow* (pages 72–73). More wittily still, the work by Vuillard entitled *Interior of the Home of Maurice Denis with 'Portrait of the Artist with the Yellow Christ' by Paul Gauguin* clearly depicts both the painting by Gauguin and the wallpaper that hung in the Denis family dining room, which can be seen in the background of the picture.

Another French painter, James Tissot, working in a more sophisticated style, filled his painted interiors with floral wallpapers, and as with the works of all of these artists, the inclusion of wallpaper had the effect of anchoring his paintings firmly in everyday life.

The Fauves go wild with colour

The Fauves also painted wallpaper. According to Matisse, 'Colour can do anything. The drawing and the colours should work together as one.' Fauvism used colour as its principal means of expression, a way of making the physical world palpable and of conveying sensation. The Fauves combined colours to increase their expressivity and occasionally drew their inspiration from wallpapers. In *The Dessert: Harmony in Red*, Matisse transforms the space of the painting into a decorative scheme, in which the bold motifs on the wallpaper and tablecloth echo one another, becoming the dominant element in the picture. His many *Odalisques* (see above) and other female subjects regularly pose in front of strong motifs that contribute to the emotional charge of the work, and in his *Interior with Aubergines*, the wallpaper has greater visual impact than the aubergines themselves. By turning it into a carefully orchestrated patchwork, Matisse's painting prefigures Picasso's monumental *Femmes à la toilette* (painted twenty-five years later) in which the

artist arranges pieces of wallpaper on the canvas, exploiting its random juxtapositions to create a *trompe l'oeil* effect. Picasso's *Man with Pipe* relies on the same technique and *Large Nude in Red Armchair* shows its subject in front of an expanse of wallpaper. Once again, the inclusion of the wallcovering serves to insert an element of everyday reality, just as Cubism had sought to do.

From collage to all-over patterns

As time went on, references to wallpaper in art became increasingly incidental. René Magritte produced some wallpaper designs early in his career and painted panoramic skies as a background to his pictures. Like Picasso and Max Ernst, the Dadaist Kurt Schwitters also incorporated fragments of wallpaper into his collages, but in an even more quirky way.

In the US, the painters of the Pattern and Decoration movement of the 1970s uniformly covered the surface of their canvases with stylized motifs surrounded by a decorative border, with no attempt to create depth or perspective. Working in direct opposition to conceptual artists, painters such as Miriam Schapiro, Valerie Jaudon, Robert R. Zakanitch and Robert Kushner adopted the use of all-over patterns in a quest for a purely visual and decorative form of art, copying the principle of repetition that is intrinsic to wallpaper.

PARIS MATCH

N° 294 Du 13 au 20 NOV. 1954 Alt. du Nord 60 fr. **50** Fr.
10 fr. Belg. — S.F. 1/6. — 0.90 Suisse. — Rome 65 fr.

NOS ENVOYÉS SPÉCIAUX DANS LE MAQUIS DE L'AURÈS

LE TESTAMENT DE MATISSE
Quelques semaines avant sa mort, celui qui fut un grand maître de la peinture contemporaine découpe des papiers de couleurs dans son atelier de Cimiez. Il a quatre-vingt-cinq ans. C'est la dernière forme de son art. Il a composé ainsi les vitraux de la chapelle de Vence qui restera son testament artistique.

Opposite: Reclining Odalisque (1926) by Henri Matisse, Metropolitan Museum of Art, New York. Matisse (1869–1954) often painted his subjects against boldly patterned backgrounds such as this one.
Above: Towards the end of his life, Matisse – shown here at the age of eighty-five – extended his artistic practice to include paper cut-outs and murals, working with motifs that were not dissimilar to wallpaper patterns.

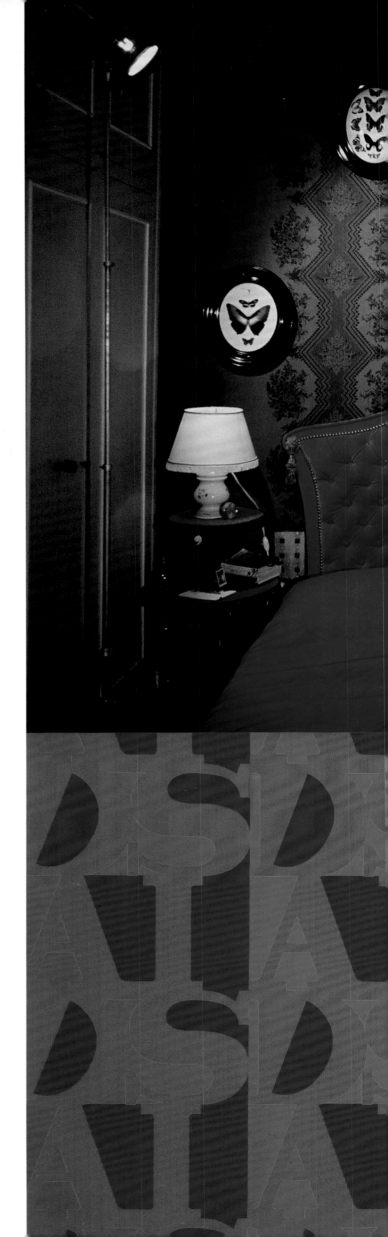

Off the wall

Andy Warhol saw wallpaper as a perfect vehicle for popular art and during the 1970s, many American conceptual artists began using this apparently innocuous medium as a means of creating their own personal and often subversive manifestos, which were splashed across the walls of museums and art galleries. In 2003, the Fabric Workshop and Museum in Philadelphia, in collaboration with the Rhode Island School of Design, held an exhibition entitled 'On the Wall: Wallpaper and Tableau', showcasing a selection of papers by postmodern artists. The show was impressive both for the number of designs featured and for its roster of designers, including John Baldessari, Mike Bidlo, Adam Cvijanovic, Drew Dominick, Nicole Eisenman, Viola Frey, General Idea, Robert Gober, Lonnie Graham, Rodney Graham, Jim Isermann, Roy Lichtenstein, Virgil Marti, Takashi Murakami, Do-Ho Suh, Rosemarie Trockel, Andy Warhol and William Wegman.

Many of these artists were inspired by the idea of subverting classic wallpaper motifs. Renée Green, for example, drew on the colours and allegorical subjects of traditional *toiles de Jouy*, while incorporating anti-colonial imagery in an attempt to encourage viewers to think about the issue of racism. Virgil Marti incorporated wallpaper into an installation as a tribute to Oscar Wilde who, as he lay dying in a hotel room, reputedly declared: 'My wallpaper is killing me. One of us will have to go.' Others used the medium of wallpaper to convey a personal or political message, such as Zineb Sedira's allusions to the duality of her Franco-Algerian identity, while some made reference to everyday domestic imagery, creating an interplay of double meanings in order to maximize our sense of unease regarding subjects like war, racism, cultural conflicts and sex. AIDS was a source of many such references during the eighties and nineties.

Above: *Photographer Sam Lévin often incorporated wallpaper into his images, as in this portrait of actress Mercedes Molinar.*
Below: *'AIDS Wallpaper' (1989), by the art collective General Idea, was just one of the designs exhibited at the Philadelphia Museum of Art in 2003. A number of contemporary wallpaper designs have been inspired by social and political issues.*

Ruling out pleasure

While teaching at Stuttgart's Academy of Visual Arts, the American conceptual artist Joseph Kosuth took over the walls of the Kubinski Gallery's three exhibition rooms to show Zero & Not — a work obsessively based around a paragraph from Sigmund Freud's Beyond the Pleasure Principle, which was printed fifteen and a half times all over the walls, then crossed out with black tape so that it was impossible to read. The result was a new kind of manifesto by an artist whose goal is to 'produce meaning' — even if doing so means banishing aesthetics and the text itself.

Warhol's wallcoverings

Andy Warhol was a visionary artist, impossible to pin down, who used his art to convey ironic messages about the world around him. Walls covered with cow's heads (page 78) or portraits of Chairman Mao (above) were ways for this New York icon to parody wallpaper and to poke fun at contemporary American interiors and their obsession with tradition. In addition to designing his own wallpaper, the master of pop art also used it as a setting for his paintings — perhaps a tribute, conscious or otherwise, to the Nabis. In 1966, Warhol showed his pink cows on a yellow ground as works in their own right at New York's Leo Castelli Gallery, and later, at the Whitney Museum of American Art, he used the same

paper in a red and purple colourway, as a backdrop for his own paintings. Some of his works are a little like wallpaper in their obsessive use of repetition and juxtaposition. One of his exhibition projects involved covering the walls of the Whitney Museum with three hundred of his **Flowers**, which was tantamount to creating a wallpaper design — a **mise en abyme** of which he himself would have been very much aware.

'When I look at things, I always see the space they occupy', said Warhol. 'My favourite piece of sculpture is a solid wall with a hole in it to frame the space on the other side.'

Above: *Andy Warhol regularly used wallpaper as a backdrop for exhibitions. This image shows the 2004 Warhol retrospective at the Museum Kunstpalast, Düsseldorf.*

Rock 'n' roll wallpaper

Pop art has always had close links with rock music. Lou Reed was a friend of Julian Schnabel and Andy Warhol's works appeared on the Velvet Underground's album covers, while Mick Jagger commissioned Warhol to create artworks for him. David Bowie began collecting works by Damien Hirst and others, but soon took the plunge himself and started creating his own art while continuing with his music career. Keen to design something that would have as wide an audience as possible, in 1995 he produced two wallpaper designs for Laura Ashley: 'British Conflict', featuring Bowie's own portrait of Lucian Freud, and 'The Crouch', depicting minotaur-like figures, whose genitals he was obliged to delete for fear of shocking too many customers. 'I chose wallpaper,' he said in an interview at the time, 'because it was incongruous, halfway between great art and minor art, an everyday art.' Bowie may well have been harking back to his working-class origins and to pub walls decorated with flock wallpaper.

Challenging tradition

In 2010 two major exhibitions focused on wallpaper designs by artists. One, 'Walls Are Talking' at Manchester's Whitworth Art Gallery, brought together works by more than thirty artists, including Andy Warhol, Sarah Lucas and Damien Hirst. Meanwhile in Switzerland, the Mudac in Lausanne and the Musée de Pully joined forces to host a major exhibition of contemporary wallpaper, the first of its kind in the country. The image of wallpaper as protective and cosy cocoon was once again swept aside by a generation of artists whose aim was to overcome the tedium of repeat motifs. Repetition itself was not the problem: it was the motifs that needed to be challenged.

Christine Tarkowski produced a design with dots created by shooting bullets through the roll of paper. Robert Gober, an artist whose works reveal his fascination for walls, designed a wallpaper whose pattern seems innocent enough from a distance, but, on closer inspection, consists of close-ups of male and female sex genitalia. Another of Gober's designs featured sleeping figures interspersed with images of a hanged man.

Damien Hirst is one of the most consciously Warholian of contemporary artists, known for playing around with optical effects, and his butterflies, while readily distinguished in close-up, become lost in an overall pattern when viewed from a distance. A design by Lisa Hecht resembled a trellis, but turned out to be an ugly chain-link fence; another, by Hayley Tompkins, resembled a pretty rose chintz but was made up from portraits of crying babies – perhaps another way of suggesting

that a home can be a prison. A wallpaper by Thomas Demand featured a pleasant pattern of intertwining ivy leaves, but was inspired by a child murderer's lair. Another design used the head of performance artist Leigh Bowery as a repeat motif, while an elegant 18th-century wallpaper was digitally altered by Francesco Simeti to include images of Afghan refugees. Fortunately, some artists had lighter messages to convey, including David Shrigley with his whimsical designs. Others were simply happy to produce continuations of their existing body of work: William Wegman, for instance, created an alphabet from traditional photographic portraits of his dogs, recalling children's bedroom wallpapers of the 1950s.

After Marcel Duchamp first exhibited a urinal as a work of art (*Fountain*, 1917), the most humble domestic objects began to find their way into museums. Now it was wallpaper's turn to welcome surreal interpretations and these two exhibitions demonstrated a contemporary art form in a bold and experimental mood, exploring the boundaries between art and design and relishing in the cross-pollination of forms.

Opposite: *Portrait of author William S. Burroughs against a wallpaper backdrop. Photograph by Wolfgang Wesener.*

Colour &

Pattern

Wallpaper is an expression of our personalities, a revelation of a particular state of mind. It is like a double that clings to us, close as a shadow, solid and yet ambiguous. Perhaps this ambiguity is what gives it its charm. Two simple elements are combined to produce an infinite range of different effects: one is pattern, the other colour. The pattern should be interesting enough to evoke an atmosphere, but not so overpowering as to eclipse the furniture and objects in a room. The whole thing is a balancing act. Its success depends on the ability of the designer to create a motif whose beauty is able to survive the process of mass reproduction. It also depends on colour, that mixture of light and alchemy that can give any reality an entirely new sheen.

Opposite: *This restaurant in Roche-sur-Yon in the Vendée region of France makes striking use of graphic patterns in psychedelic shades.*
Previous pages: *'Love Today' by Myrine Créations.*

Illusions of grandeur

How can a repeated motif avoid the risk of seeming repetitive? This is one of the great mysteries and difficulties of wallpaper design. It's a delicate task to find the right balance between a virtually non-existent design that leaves the walls looking bland, and a motif that is too oppressive, making its presence felt too strongly. This problem has existed since the days of domino papers, with their geometric or floral patterns packed together within a confined space. Once it became the norm to join the dominos together to form long rolls, the motif had more space to breathe.

The art of imitation

From an early date, one of the principal roles of the motif was to create the illusion of something else. At the begininng, wallpaper was always a substitute for more expensive materials: it imitated wood or marble, and later, as printing techniques grew more advanced, it could become a cheaper replacement for fabric draperies. Less expensive than silk, lighter than stucco, it became the master of illusion.

This illusion was deliberate, however, since everyone was a party to it and indeed, illusion was sometimes valued more highly than reality: in its heyday, Réveillon wallpaper could cost as much as silk. The idea was to capture the 'feel' of the material rather than its physical reality, and new technology was often driven by this desire for counterfeiture. Iridescent paper, for example, was designed to imitate silk, while flock paper imitated devoré velvet and damasks, and it was in order to reproduce the look of Cordoban leather that the technique of embossing was developed.

Making life more beautiful

Nonetheless, a day came when motifs stopped trying to imitate other materials and developed a life of their own. After that, every era had its own decorative ideas. The earliest motifs were floral. Then architectural designs began to adorn the entrance halls and drawing rooms of grand houses. In the 17th century, exploiting advances in technology, artists and the more imaginative manufacturers began imitating patterns other than those of fabric or leather, and in the 18th century Réveillon and his imitators used distemper colour to produce arabesques and allegorical and neoclassical motifs. Subsequent designs involved vases of flowers, columns, busts and statues, and even reconstructions of entire gardens in a *trompe l'oeil* style. In the 19th century, wallpaper drew inspiration from every field of human endeavour: professions, politics, the army, mythology, industry and more. Motifs appeared that were inspired by the construction of the railways and the invention of the Zeppelin, by the adventurous expeditions of Alexander von Humboldt, David Livingstone or Vitus Bering, and all the stories that were told about them, and by distant lands such as China and Japan, which spawned a host of large-scale exotic motifs showing scenes from everyday life, birds and figures. But the second half of the 19th century abandoned this human element and returned its focus to nature.

'Beware of imitations'

'Beware, for example, of those coarse and vulgar imitations of tapestry, those felts that have been dyed and glued, which foreign countries, particularly England, have been trying to import into France! Beautiful wallpaper is a thousand times preferable, and is currently acquiring a level of perfection that appears difficult to surpass. The danger for the wallpaper industry, from the point of view of taste, relates to its very perfection. Indeed, intoxicated by the success of their imitations, manufacturers have reached a point where they are attempting to imitate actual paintings...'

Le Journal des Demoiselles, 1867

Wallpaper has long been used to create illusions.
Opposite: Wallpaper decorated with imitation drapery (1893), Musée du Papier Peint, Rixheim.
This page, background: A lace-inspired contemporary design by French firm Intérieurs & Dépendance.
This page, left: A trompe l'oeil wallpaper panel (1895), machine printed by David Walker & Co.

'All those delightful birds are handpainted'

'At Maigret's house, Mme de Forget and I saw a Chinese paper used as wallpaper. He told us that French art was quite incapable of producing a colour as solid as this or even approaching it. He tried to colour in a section of the pink background, but apparently it looked dreadful in no time at all.

The paper is relatively inexpensive. All those delightful birds are handpainted and he told us that the decorative flourishes are all bamboo stalks, pale coloured with little touches of silver, filling in the background, which is pink and perfectly uniform; the whole thing is scattered with birds and butterflies. It is perfect and charming, not because of any tiny inexactitude in the imitation, as is always the case with French decoration; no, it was the whole thing, the graceful composition and the contrasting colours, all rendered with a witty lightness that was embodied in the subject in such a way as to turn that quality itself into a form of decorative ornament, like the animals in Egyptian monuments and manuscripts.'

Eugène Delacroix, *Journal*, 9 October 1847

Inspired by antiquity

In the 18th century, it was fashionable for painters, printmakers, architects and young men from wealthy families to travel through Europe and experience for themselves the birthplaces of Mediterranean art. Greek and Roman remains were a huge source of inspiration, and the rediscovery of Pompeii in 1749 played a key role in the rise of neoclassicism, which came to influence every field of the arts, including fashion. Designers working for the French royal wallpaper manufacturers, Réveillon and Arthur, drew heavily on the neoclassical style, creating landscapes, statues and colonnades.

Previous page, left: *This 19th-century American paper looks strikingly modern.*
Previous page, right: *Design by Dufour et Leroy (1822–40) inspired by La Fontaine's* Fables, *blockprinted in fifteen iridescent colours on a satin ground.*

Some wallpaper designs draw their inspiration from history, others from the contemporary world of industry.
Above: *English neoclassical* trompe l'oeil *paper used in the 1769 redecoration of a manor house in Bourton-on-the-Water, Gloucestershire.*
Right: *View of a railway station, a design by Potters of Darwen, Lancashire, 1853.*

Sophisticated touches

'Not content with producing imitations of plain fabrics, manufacturers came up with the inspiring idea of imitating velvet and brocade fabrics… Rather than simply gilding the paper or producing a velvety finish, they attempted to give it the same relief and the same texture as the fabric itself, so that the illusion would be complete. On expensive wallpapers, they usually added a number of sophisticated touches that completed the impression of a true trompe l'oeil. We can safely say that there were no clever subterfuges, subtle techniques or ingenious ideas to which manufacturers did not resort during that era.'

Henri Havard, *Dictionary of Furnishing and Decoration*, Paris, 1890

Left: *'Damask Ladies',
a modern take on
damask by illustrator
Jordi Labanda for the
Spanish firm Coordonné.*

The fall and rise of the motif

Wallpaper has always been inextricably linked
with the evolution of art and taste, and in the
20th century it reflected the aesthetic upheavals
that went hand in hand with social change. As
its relationship with architectural spaces became
increasingly central, ornamental patterns gave
way to the geometric shapes typical of Art Deco,
but abstraction was already making inroads,
anticipating the total disappearance of the motif
advocated by the Bauhaus. Modernist design
favoured simple effects that could be achieved
through materials alone – an approach better
suited to small interiors and the demands of social
housing, which were a major market at the time.

The motif made its triumphant reappearance
in the wake of the Second World War – although
there was little to applaud in terms of quality.
The abiding image from the 1950s is of whimsical
geometric patterns made up of a mixture of
vertical lines, zigzags and circles and bright,
childlike designs, while the 1970s are associated
with Vasarely-style graphic shapes, lurid motifs
and psychedelic flowers.

Breaking down boundaries

Today's wallpaper industry makes its profits
wherever it can, offering contemporary designs
alongside firmly traditional motifs. Damasks,
florals and stripes are reinterpreted in different
materials and colours to achieve varied effects.
Every country has its own preferences: the British
have always loved little flowers, Regency stripes and
embossed effects; the Germans have a penchant for
faux finishes and padded papers; the Scandinavians
prefer geometric patterns and Gustavian stripes,
while the French maintain their reputation as
specialists in damasks and lush flower designs.
But globalization is sweeping aside geographical
frontiers, and styles now travel the globe at the
speed of light: modern Japanese interiors, papered
with damasks and arabesques, are a case in point.

What all the designers have in common is
that they are required to take risks, think big and
stick to their guns. Whether we are talking full-
blown florals, architectural structures in *toile de
Jouy* style, 1970s-inspired geometrics or Art Deco
extravagances, the important thing is scale. And
scale is much easier once wallpaper becomes virtual,
with resizeable motifs and video systems that allow
a design to be projected on to a wall and changed
at will. Réveillon would be amazed.

Close relations

Wallpaper and textiles have always been close relations, swapping motifs as if it were the most natural thing in the world, although textiles have always led the way in the development of motifs, perhaps because continuous patterns are easier to achieve on fabric.

In the 17th century, the manufacturers of the wonderful printed calicoes known as indiennes, inspired by traditional Indian textiles, transposed their motifs onto wallpaper, and in the 18th century Réveillon and Oberkampf, founder of the toile de Jouy workshops, helped one another out seasonally, as the need arose, with exchanges of manpower and technical skill. The major graphic artists associated with the Arts and Crafts and Art Deco movements also readily moved back and forth between textiles and wallpaper. In the UK, Lucienne Day, Laura Ashley and Tricia Guild were all textile designers before transferring their visual ideas to wallpaper, and the same is true for Zofia Rostad and Paule Marrot in France.

Today, firms such as Nobilis, Sanderson and Pierre Frey produce matching ranges of textiles and wallpaper, and most recently the French firm Braquenié has launched a wallpaper collection inspired by its fabrics.

Matching wallpapers and textiles have long been popular. These designs are 'Primavera' from Sanderson (above left) and 'Fairhaven' by Jane Churchill (opposite).

Classic motifs – arabesques, flowers, damasks and medallions – provide contemporary designers with endless potential for reinvention.
Above: *'YSW Decenio' by Spanish firm Ybarra & Serret.*
Opposite: *'Hummingbirds' by British manufacturer Cole & Son.*

Timeless trends

Some motifs are still as fresh today as when they were first created by the great designers of the 18th century, and many wallpaper classics continue to adorn our walls, some having barely changed over the centuries.

Floral fantasies

Flowers are a timeless motif, ranging from the fresh and delicate to the luscious and luxuriant. The slightly clumsy blooms of the early dominos reappeared, scattered lightly over chintzes, curved in Oriental style over printed calicoes and dusted with velvet pile on the early flock papers. After the French Revolution, floral motifs became less stylized and were rendered in naturalistic, almost botanical fashion. The Arts and Crafts movement gave them sweeping, dynamic curves; Alphonse Mucha's lively and fantastical designs relied heavily on the poppy motif, with its associations with opium and social excess, while Art Deco produced a veritable explosion of flowers. The 1960s brought a new freedom, with the rise of Scandinavian design, with its beautiful large blooms in vivid colours, and the nostalgic English florals of Laura Ashley. And of course, flowers continue to feature in most major collections today. Manuel Canovas, a great garden lover and an enthusiastic traveller, is one of the big names associated with them, while Tricia Guild perpetuates the English tradition in her vibrant acid palette.

Arabesques

Swirling arabesque motifs, originally copied from silk textiles, were one of the 18th century's dominant decorative themes and were versatile enough to suit almost any interior. Contemporary designers still look to the arabesque for inspiration: it features in a number of ultra-modern designs from the Italian firm Jannelli & Volpi and French studio Munchausen, while Belgian designer Agnès Emery incorporates her own version into her beautiful dominos.

Eastern inspiration

Chinese paper was first brought to the western world by the East India Companies. It is believed that it was not originally sold, but offered as a gift to mark a successful trade deal or secure a contract.

But these gorgeous mulberry-fibre papers painted with gouache or tempera, with designs that were devoid of light and shade or perspective, rapidly became a source of widespread admiration. The English came up with the idea of reproducing them by bringing Chinese artists over to London to produce wallpapers in which the refinement of the Chinese style was adapted for western tastes. Many European and American artists began to draw on the Chinese decorative repertoire and used motifs such as pagodas, dragons, trees and birds to depict a fanciful version of China, as recreated through the western imagination. The chinoiserie craze even extended to architects, who dotted Chinese pavilions across parks and landscape gardens, including the Désert de Retz in Chambourcy, France, or the grounds of the Sans-Souci palace in Potsdam, Germany.

Chinoiserie motifs are still popular today. In 2005, Tim Butcher and his wife Lizzie Deshayes set up a company producing handmade silk wallpaper based on designs by talented Chinese artists. Combining luxury materials with an immaculate finish, Fromental seeks to blend Oriental classicism with city chic, creating a contemporary look through imaginative reinterpretations of traditional Chinese styles (page 230).

Above: *'Wisteria' by Anna French.*
Opposite, inset: *From left to right, a floral design by Colefax and Fowler, 'Early Tulips' by Sanderson and 'Watelet' by Designers Guild.*

Arabesque admiration

'In Paris now, almost the only paper being used to decorate drawing room walls is the variety patterned with arabesques... Why choose arabesques? Perhaps because they are lighter and less visually demanding; because they have a particularly clear, concise form; and because they can either be linked or separate according to one's preference, and can easily be placed inside a frame of any size that one chooses.'

Magasin des Modes Nouvelles Françaises et Anglaises, 18 May 1788

Above: *'Anakreon' by GoHome, a damask pattern with a very contemporary feel.*
Right: *A design from the* Lotus Papers *range by Farrow & Ball, inspired by 19th-century French motifs.*

Opposite: *'Petit Parc' and 'Peinture' wallpapers by Braquenié create an opulent feel.*
This page: *'Hummingbirds' by Cole & Son adorns the Paul Smith store on Boulevard Raspail, Paris.*

Stripes

There are stripes to suit every mood – from discreetly drawn pinstripes to the broad and exuberant deckchair stripes – and there are very few wallpaper collections in which they do not feature. Designers are constantly inventing new stripe variations in different colour combinations or creating playful interiors by using them horizontally as well as vertically. Stripes can be deployed in a small area or they can determine the total look of a room. They can be vivacious or calming; they can make a room seem wider or taller, endlessly juggling with our perception of space.

Ralph Lauren, the icon of New England chic, specializes in stripes in elegant, muted colours: Ralph Lauren wallpapers are the choice of movie set designers who want to recreate the stylish and relaxed ambiance of the apartments of New York's Lower East Side. Another lover of stripes, French fashion designer Jean-Charles de Castelbajac, chooses to fill the walls with an exuberant multicoloured version (see right).

Coqui Ybarra, founder and artistic director of the Spanish design house Ybarra & Serret, uses stripes drawn freehand in a distinctive range of watercolour shades: sky blue, eau de nil, raspberry and slate grey, together with silver. But perhaps the maestros of stripes are British paint and wallpaper specialists Farrow & Ball. The firm produces a wealth of stripe variations – 'Block Print Stripe', 'Broad Stripe', 'Closet Stripe', 'Plain Stripe' and more – all of them available in a range of soft and subtle colourways.

Right: *'Sing Sing', a cheerful stripe by Jean-Charles de Castelbajac for Lutèce.*
Overleaf, left: *'Haufenweise', a Single-Tapete design in a typically bold colourway.*
Overleaf, right: *'Wallpaper No. 2' by David Hicks, on show in the David Hicks France store in Paris.*
Page 116: *'Florentina', a delicate floral by Swedish brand Sandberg.*
Page 117: *'Orlando', a handcrafted design from the Parisian studio Dominos, using traditional techniques and natural pigments.*

Colour codes

An early wallpaper workshop had the air of an alchemist's den, but the goal of the craftmen who worked there was not gold but colour. First, printer's inks were mixed with oil. Then distemper colours were created by binding pigments together with glue. From the 18th century onwards, efforts were focused on expanding the colour palette and breaking away from the dull greys and browns of the early dominos. Larger manufacturers employed specialist colourmakers to develop shades that were unique to each firm; the recipes remained a closely guarded secret, and there was enormous competition to see who could obtain the best spring green, chrome green, yellow ochre, cobalt blue or deep crimson. Prussian blue was first discovered in Switzerland. Scientific research undertaken by Robert Dossie and Michel-Eugène Chevreul demonstrated that the complexity of colours actually has more to do with optics than with chemistry, and that the proximity of different colours to one another influences our visual perception: to achieve the desired results, therefore, it was as important to consider these optical effects as the dyes themselves. 'Every wallpaper...should have a border, generally darker and more complex in terms of pattern and colour than the paper it serves to frame', advised Chevreul in his treatise *The Principles of Harmony and Contrast of Colours* (1839).

A palette for every period

As well as inventing new colours, it was important to use existing ones creatively. One example of this was Jean Zuber's experiments with iridescence, a reflective effect that produced a shifting rainbow of colours. Following industrial advances at the beginning of the 19th century, machines could soon print in six, eight and eventually twenty-four and twenty-eight colours. But even this was nothing when compared with the artistry of the handprinted panoramas, which used up to two hundred and fifty colours to produce incomparable effects of depth and luminosity. French makers used water-based pigments that produced a matt effect, while the British used distemper colours, which had greater brilliance. Manufacturers also competed over ways to fix the colours and prevent fading. And successfully so: when we admire the antique wallpapers still hanging in grand homes or carefully conserved in museums, it is astonishing to see how the colours have retained their brightness. They are like Sleeping Beauties awoken after more than a century, still as fresh as a rose.

Every era has its own colour codes. Early classical motifs, geometric friezes and flower garlands were in subdued, matt shades. Then came powder pink, pale yellow, sky blue and olive green, followed by an explosion of colour inspired by the works of 20th-century artists, from Marie Laurencin to Andy Warhol via Paul Poiret, Jacques-Émile Ruhlmann, Léonor Fini and Henri Matisse. The psychedelic post-war years gave pride of place to purples, oranges and reds, while Pop art brought a train of grey, black and mauve, before the strict geometric lines of the 1980s embraced white, grey and beige. Today, major wallpaper brands can still be identified by their distinctive colour palettes. The colours of Élitis are explosive. David Hicks's are bold (right). Karim Rashid's are flashy, Jane Churchill's soft and creamy, Cole & Son's sophisticated, Sandberg's subtle (overleaf). Tricia Guild favours bright acid shades (page 190) and Emily Todhunter chooses dreamy pastels.

Domino delights

Describing the history of the domino manufacturing workshops in Rouen in the 16th and 17th centuries, Georges Dubosc marvels at the colours that were used:

'Everything was dependent on the colouring, those joyful, exuberant colours so pleasing to children, to simple people, to the masses! The colours of the old images were always fresh, cheerful and pleasing. There were never any false or garish colours among them. False colours, insipid mauves and blues, did not appear until 1880, with the chemical aniline-based dyes. The colours...were restricted. There were only red, blue, yellow and brown, and also a pale red known as **rosette**. Purple and green were obtained by printing one colour on top of another. The dyes were kept in stone pots. Brown was obtained from the buckthorn plant, **rosette** from brazil wood and brown from sienna clay, and gum arabic was used to bind the colours. The colouring of these popular images was done using a stencil and big, thick, tightly packed brushes for spreading the dye.

The stencils were made of card of sufficient thickness not to warp when the wet brush was passed over it. And since the manufacture of the stencils was a long and difficult process, so as not to have to repeat it, they were hardened with a coating of burnt oil and litharge. The dominos were strung across the workshop to dry, and all those sheets, like so many brightly coloured little flags, created a bright and cheerful scene.'

Georges Dubosc, 'L'Imagerie populaire à Rouen', *Le Journal de Rouen*, 1926

'A very big affair'

'The purchasing of the paper turned out especially to be
a very big affair. Gervaise wanted a grey paper with blue
flowers, so as to enliven and brighten the walls. Boche
offered to take her to the dealers, so that she might make
her own selection. But the landlord had given him formal
instructions not to go beyond the price of fifteen sous a
piece. They were there an hour. The laundress kept looking
in despair at a very pretty chintz pattern costing eighteen
sous a piece, and thought all the other papers hideous.
At length the concierge gave in...'

Émile Zola, *L'Assommoir*, 1877

Opposite: *'Leaf'*
by Jocelyn Warner.
Above: *'Kasbah'*
by Clarke & Clarke.

Global

Style

At the beginning of the industrial era, there were just two contenders locked in a battle for world supremacy in the field of wallpaper production – France and Great Britain. Then the dawn of the 20th century saw production take off globally. France remained a frontrunner for elegance and chic, but British designers were the most adventurous. Then, in the period between the wars, the Germans also began to make their mark, enlisting the support of major contemporary artists, and today Germany is a leading producer, with the huge Russian market conveniently located on its doorstep. Although originally slower to embrace wallpaper than Europe, the US and Canada have long since made up for any lost ground. The Scandinavian countries were relatively quick off the mark and introduced some genuine design innovations. Italy, on the other hand, continued to prefer paint to paper for many years, but it is now the home of a number of luxury brands. Spain, predictably enough, began producing designs that would have looked at home in an Almódovar film, while the Russians, rather than manufacturing wallpapers, have generally opted to buy them in instead. Wallpaper, it seems, is as varied as any other aspect of global culture.

Opposite: *'Liljekonvalj' (Lily of the Valley) by Sandberg.*
Previous pages: *'Chinoise' by Basso & Brooke, for Graham & Brown.*

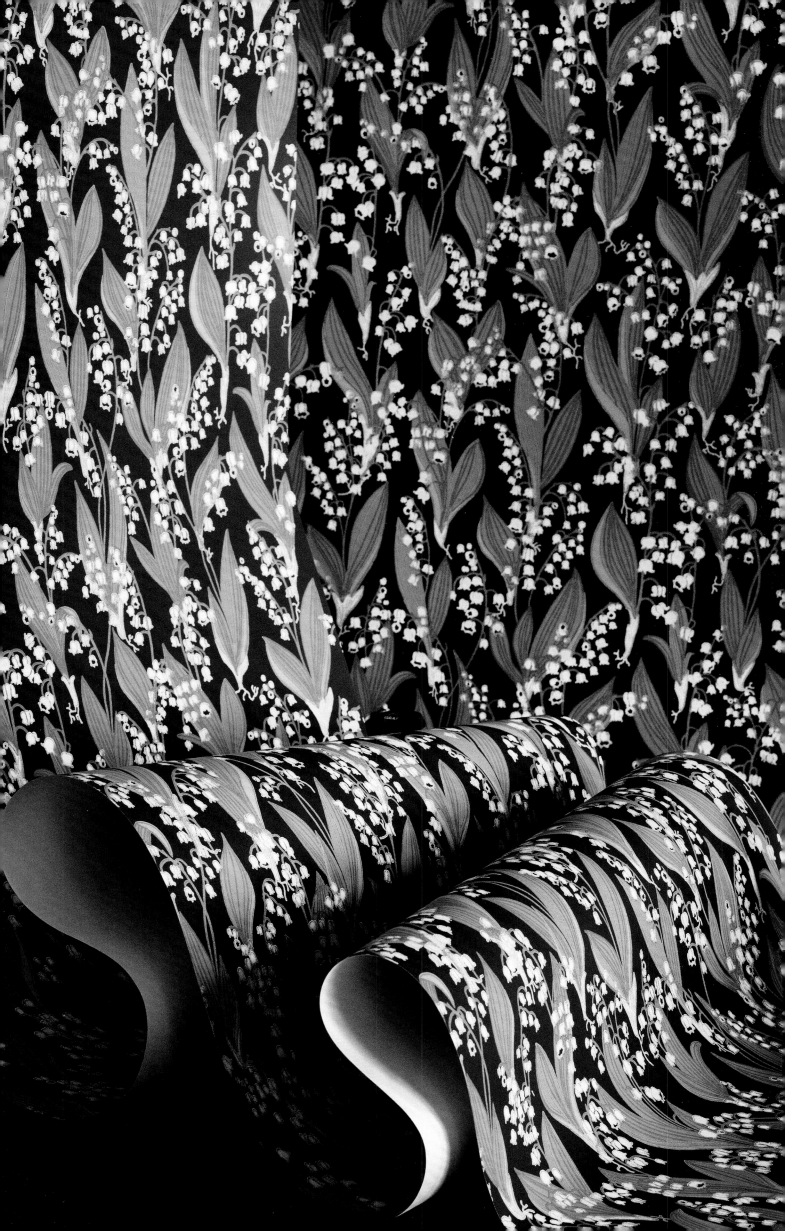

Wallpaper: a world tour

France and Belgium

The French are the heirs to the great classical tradition associated with the wallpaper-makers of Paris's Faubourg Saint-Antoine and they continue to create some of the world's most sophisticated wallcoverings. For many years, France was a centre for mass-produced wallpaper, from companies that included Vénilia, Inaltera and Essef. Many of the big French firms, however, have been forced to cut back on production or to close altogether. The firm Leroy – founded in 1846 in Paris by Louis Isidore Leroy, and later relocated to Saint-Fargeau-Ponthierry – was a major European manufacturer, but was unable to survive the economic crisis of the early eighties and closed down in 1982. Essef, another heavyweight, held out until 2009. These giants made way for new firms such as Déco France, Caselio, Ugepa and Decoralis, which operate on a global scale. Other newcomers include L'Éditeur, which exports to Russia, the upmarket brand Texam, and Lutèce, which offers an exhaustive range of styles and collaborates with designers such as Zofia Rostad and the cheekily playful Jean-Charles Castelbajac (pages 70–71). Casamance, founded in 2000, produces beautiful wallpapers in classic styles (see above), and exports them worldwide. An offshoot of the firm, Camengo, founded in 2005, aims to combine luxury with affordability and adopts a more relaxed approach than its parent company, experimenting with

colour and metallic or pearlized effects, producing panoramas and revamping classic designs.

France has also led the way in terms of a more intimate scale of operation, with family businesses focusing on top-of-the-range products. Besson and Nobilis were pioneers in this field, opening Paris's first interior design shops dedicated to wallpaper in the 1920s. Besson showed a selection of high-quality designs and Nobilis, founded by Adolphe Halard in 1928, was soon associated with top designers including Suzanne Fontan, Paule Marrot and René Gabriel, selling their designs in its store on the Rue Bonaparte. While extending its operations worldwide, the firm has stayed close to its artistic roots. Now in the hands of Adolphe Halard's son Denis, Nobilis offers a magnificent classic range, but also produces adaptations of more traditional designs, including shimmering arabesques and spectacular screenprinted *toiles de Jouy*, as well as exploring the world of contemporary motifs with the quirky *Maestro* collection.

In 1935, Pierre Frey, himself a designer, began collaborating with well-known artists to create innovative designs that employed an unusually wide range of colours for the time. His son has continued the Frey tradition, retaining a place for his father's beautiful original designs and for a handful of traditional classics, encapsulating a particularly French approach to the art of living. Pierre Frey wallpapers – which include a recent

Undiscovered gems

Élitis — which celebrated its twentieth anniversary in 2010 — is the most cosmopolitan of French wallpaper brands. Its studio views the contemporary home as a crossroads of multiple influences and draws inspiration from every corner of the globe. Élitis wallpapers are designed to transform our homes into precious jewel cases, bringing the walls to life with an endless interplay of colour and light: its flocks, pearly finishes, veneers, metallic inks, glass droplets and shimmering stripes are a celebration of sheer joie de vivre.

Nobilis was founded in Paris in 1928 by Adolphe Halard, as one of the first dedicated wallpaper stores, and still produces luxury wallpapers and fabrics today, including the two designs shown here. The company is now run by Halard's son Denis and a two-hundred-strong team, and regularly collaborates with established designers.

design by Clara Halter – are now handmade in the US and could almost pass for fabrics, so exquisite are their textures and colours. Braquenié, a brand renowned for its gorgeous textile designs, joined the Pierre Frey group in 1991, and Frey recently launched a collection of sumptuous handprinted wallpapers inspired by Braquenié's historic collections of cashmeres and calico prints.

Manuel Canovas is another designer whose name is most associated with textiles. Canovas, a great lover of gardens and a keen traveller, founded his company in 1963 and his handful of wallpaper designs featuring exotic flowers are still among the classics of their kind.

Belgium also has a strong wallpaper tradition. Following in the footsteps of Grandeco, Heytens is a leading brand, opening its first shop in Overijse in 1974 and proving so successful that other branches soon followed in Belgium and France by the mid-1990s. Arte are another market leader, as are Omexco, which began as a firm exporting luxury wallcoverings to the Middle and Far East, then decided to launch its own range and rapidly made its mark as an innovator. Its collections are notable for their luxurious tone-on-tone fabric effects (see right), their use of materials such as mica, silk and viscose thread, and gold and silver beading, and their spectacular sheen.

The United Kingdom

The British have been pioneers in wallpaper design since its earliest days. Queen Victoria is said to have taken a close interest in the choice of wallpaper for her various residences, insisting on identical colours and patterns – perhaps to ensure that she would feel at home in all of them. And British designers, traditionally regarded as the most innovative, have always had a talent for balancing quirkiness with tradition and a hint of wit.

Sanderson is one of the most internationally renowned of British brands. The firm was founded in London in 1860 as an importer of French wallpaper, but began to commission original designs in the late 1860s and built its own factory in 1879. Its papers were the work of designers including Christopher Dresser, George Haite and, most notably, C. F. A. Voysey, a magnificent Art Nouveau designer, decorative artist and architect, who also designed a new factory for the company in 1902. A pioneer of colour advertising from 1911 onwards, Sanderson was awarded a Royal Warrant as Purveyors of Wallpapers to King George V in 1923,

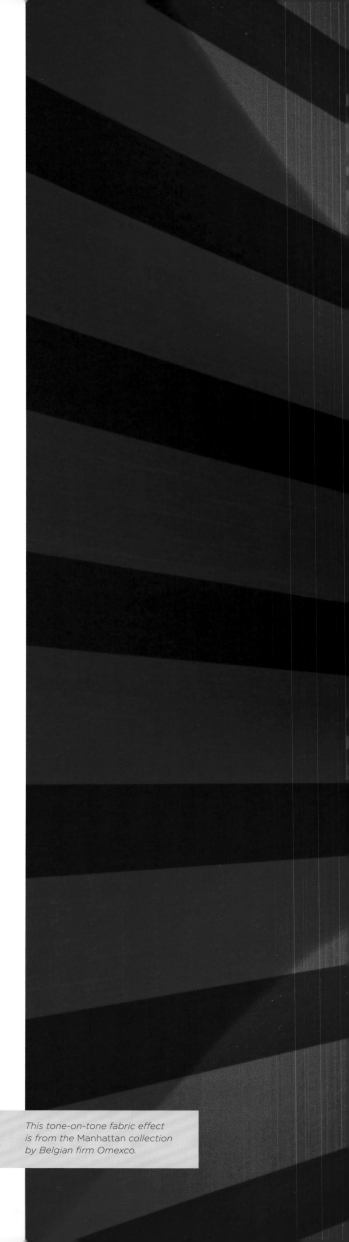

This tone-on-tone fabric effect is from the Manhattan collection by Belgian firm Omexco.

New British designers

Brands such as Mulberry, Prestigious Textiles and Little Greene Paint Company are all relatively recent additions to the rolecall of wallpaper history, although these firms were already well established elsewhere in the field of design. Tom Dixon, head of design and later creative director at Habitat, launched the 'Very Important Products' range in 2004, which has included wallpaper designs by Orla Kiely, Eley Kishimoto, Matthew Williamson, Roland Mouret and Barbara Hulanicki.

The British wallpaper scene continues to be dynamic and young designers are constantly emerging, creating idiosyncratic styles linked by a common thread of bold imagination. Popular brands and designers include Crowson, Brian Yates, Laurence Llewelyn-Bowen, Sophie Conran for Arthouse, G.P. & J. Baker, the whimsical Erica Wakerly, the witty Lewis & Wood and the eccentric Nono, while the charismatic David Oliver has already forged a reputation based on his subtle colour range, small motifs and elegant tone-on-tone prints.

and began to license motifs from Disney Studios in the 1930s. It also bought up other firms including Rottmann, Strome & Co., Charles Knowles, Turnbull & Stockdale and – most significantly – Morris and Co. in 1940, thereby acquiring all the printing blocks and pattern books belonging to the great William Morris, philosopher, designer and father of the 19th-century Arts and Crafts movement. The last member of the Sanderson family left the business in 1965 and it was bought by the Walker Greenbank group. The brand, which celebrated its 150th anniversary in 2010, has long been associated with upmarket elegance in a vivid and sophisticated colour palette, and has always remained faithful to the English country style.

Graham & Brown was established in the aftermath of the Second World War by two friends, Harold Graham and Henry Brown, both of whom were passionate about new printing technology. Harold Graham died in 1951, but the company continued to expand with financial backing from the founders' sons, and by the 1970s it was producing millions of rolls of wallpaper, becoming one of the top independent manufacturers in the UK. The third generation forged creative links with interior designer Laurence Llewelyn-Bowen, as well as Linda Barker, Marcel Wanders (pages 134–135), Wayne Hemingway, Basso & Brooke (page 120–121) and, more recently, designer Kelly Hoppen and fashion icon Barbara Hulanicki. This dynamic company has even organized competitions in art schools as a means of recruiting new design talent and has built close links with the fashion

world by selling its products through retail chains such as Monsoon. Its website offers a host of different wallcoverings, including 'wall jewels' for a customized look, and an 'eco' range that is manufactured without the use of harmful chemicals and printed on paper from managed sources.

Osborne & Little also grew up out of a friendship, this time between two brothers-in-law, Peter Osborne and Antony Little, who started out with a small showroom in Chelsea in 1968 and went on to build the Osborne & Little empire thanks to their award-winning first collection of handprinted wallpapers. The firm has expanded its product range to include fabrics, trimmings, accessories and furniture, creating complete interiors in which everything complements everything else. For the last forty years, Osborne & Little creations have occupied a central place in the world of interior design, from the paint effects of the 1980s to the current metallic trends, via the sun, moon and star motifs of the 1990s. Osborne & Little have also begun distributing designs by Nina Campbell and the Parisian design studio Lorca. What all of these wallpapers have in common is a fresh colour palette and what might be described as a poetic approach to pattern.

Colefax and Fowler – the creation of John Fowler, Sibyl Colefax and Nancy Lancaster – were founded on London's Fulham Road and for the last fifty years have embodied the essence of English style, that sense of timeless elegance that is so characteristic of modern British interiors and which blends comfort, a restrained palette and relaxed informality. Colefax and Fowler also market the work of other design talents, including Manuel Canovas and the highly original work of Jane Churchill (page 103), whose fresh and relaxed designs seem quintessentially British.

A riot of flowers and insects.
Opposite: *'Rose Chinoise' by Colefax and Fowler.*
Above: *'Nakai' by Boussac from Pierre Frey.*

Cole & Son: cutting-edge classicism

This old family firm, a byword for British design and bohemian elegance, belongs to the exclusive club of suppliers to the British royal family. Founded in 1873 by John Perry, the son of a vicar, the company — then known as John Perry Ltd — was based in Islington in north London, an area famous for its printing firms. The factory then moved to Haringey, a few miles north of its original site, while the showroom was situated in fashionable Chelsea. The company retains the same spirit today, employing skilled craftspeople and combining traditional processes invented by John Perry with the latest in modern technology.

When Perry died, in 1940, the factory and its archive of wooden printing blocks were bought by a successful wallpaper merchant by the name of A. P. Cole. Cole & Son had the foresight to seek out other collections of printing blocks and acquire them when they came up for sale, notably those of J. C. Crace and Son, a company that had printed wallpapers for numerous stately homes, palaces and theatres in England and overseas, including Pugin's designs for the Palace of Westminster. In 1949, in response to the revolution in contemporary design, Cole created one of the first screenprint studios in Europe and began collaborating with a number of artists, including Lucienne Day, Peggy Argus, John Drummond and Eduardo Paolozzi.

Today, the Cole & Son archive contains some 1,800 blockprint designs, 350 screenprint designs and a huge number of original drawings, including styles from the 18th, 19th and early 20th centuries. Among these are original wallpaper designs for a number of historic houses, including Buckingham Palace and the White House. This magnificent archive is the major source of all new Cole & Son collections. Designs are carefully selected and adapted by the firm's design studio to produce wallpapers that have a contemporary feel while remaining faithful to the spirit of their source. Designs by Mackintosh, Voysey and Vasarely are regularly retrieved from the archives and given a new lease of life, while contemporary names including David Easton, Tom Dixon and the fashion designer Vivienne Westwood (see right) have also been invited to collaborate.

Above: 'Il Sole', a design by Piero Fornasetti for Cole & Son.
Right: Three Vivienne Westwood papers, also for Cole & Son.

A passion for paper

Carole Texier has always been an ardent champion of wallpaper, possibly because her mother, Monique Martin, founder of the famous Dominotiers firm in Paris, instilled in her a love of wallpaper from the earliest age. In 1993, a time when wallpaper was out of favour with interior designers, the adventurous Texier dared to start her own business, opening a showroom where creativity was anything but an empty word. Au Fil des Couleurs became something of a landmark, a place where top interior decorators, theatre and movie designers, along with ordinary customers, came flocking in search of a rare gem. In December 2009, Frank Halard, spiritual heir to another famous wallpaper brand and a leading figure in the world of interior design, took over the reins of the firm, and with it the tireless quest for pattern, texture and colour. Halard is a great lover of the beautiful and the unusual and can be implicitly trusted to safeguard and enrich a collection that already boasts more than ten thousand wallpaper designs. Whether the papers are digitally printed or blockprinted by hand, what matters to Halard is that the results should be supremely beautiful. He has now signed exclusive contracts with the Swedish firm Sandberg and also with Cole & Son in the UK, making him the first French stockist of designs such as those by Vivienne Westwood (see above).

'Stella' (this page) and 'Grace' (opposite) are two designs from a flamboyant collection by celebrated Dutch designer Marcel Wanders in association with Graham & Brown, using a combination of matt paper and iridescent inks.

Channel crossings

The French and the British both claim to have invented wallpaper, and remain keen competitors in this as in so many other matters. In the 17th century, the French were still deeply suspicious of their northern neighbours after eight centuries of rivalry. Following the revocation of the Edict of Nantes, the flight of the Protestant Huguenots to 'Perfidious Albion' — taking with them their printing skills — gave the British a distinct advantage, and they subsequently went on to invent flocking, continuous paper, distemper colour, and — most revolutionary of all — mechanized printing. But France rallied, thanks to the genius of Réveillon, Dufour and Zuber and their ilk, and Paris reclaimed the high ground, improving on its neighbour's techniques and becoming, during the Empire, the artistic hub of Europe and, during the Second Empire, the capital of good taste. France continued to dominate European production until the end of the 19th century, and a columnist writing about the Universal Exhibition held in Paris in 1844 commented on the export of wallpaper, which had doubled in volume over ten years: 'There is no competition where this article is concerned and French taste continues to influence it entirely.'

It was not until the free trade agreement signed by France and the United Kingdom in 1860 that tensions subsided — at least, to a degree. For some time, France remained unrivalled in the production of luxury wallpapers. But in the 1960s, the era of Swinging London, the spotlight was directed once more across the Channel, where the likes of David Hicks and Laura Ashley were championing the British creative spirit, inspiring a long line of designers that followed. And so the battle rages on.

Germany

They may not have the same historical tradition
of wallpaper manufacture as the French and the
British, but over the last fifty years the Germans
have become heavyweights within the industry.
There was no lull in wallpaper production in
Germany in the 1980s as there was elsewhere,
and German firms are still forging new ground:
Erismann has opened a factory in Russia,
while A.S. Création has launched a wallpaper
competition called 'New Walls, Please!', in order
to unearth new design talent.

German manufacturers now successfully
combine a huge turnover with constant innovation.
Back in the autumn of 1929, Dr Emil Rasch
began to sell a Bauhaus collection, designed in
collaboration with the famous school of art in
Dessau. Rasch purchased the rights to the Bauhaus
name from Mies van der Rohe and regularly
reissues these timeless and elegantly simple designs
by updating the colour palette (pages 40–41).
Then in the 1950s, Rasch began to collaborate
with designers Margret Hildebrand and Lucienne

Day, the painter Tea Ernst, the Frenchman Jean
de Botton, and even the artist Salvador Dalí
(pages 76–77).

Rasch found further collaborative success
in 1992 with the *Zeitwände* collection, created by
designers and architects of international standing
including Berghof/Landes/Rang, Ginbande
Design, Wolfgang Laubersheimer, Alessandro
Mendini, Nathalie du Pasquier, George J. Sowden
and Matteo Thun. The Italian architect Ettore
Sottsass and his famous Memphis Group also
contributed to the collection, which was won a
number of awards and was exhibited in major
museums. Czech architect and designer Borek
Sipek was acclaimed for his embossed paper
adorned with glass beads, while the prolific Markus
Benesch has also collaborated with Rasch as well
as with Italian firm Jannelli e Volpi. Today, Rasch
sells papers by artists such as Barbara Becker (pages
140–141), as well as the glow-in-the-dark designs
of French duo Ich & Kar (pages 182–183).

The company Marburg has now been making
wallcoverings for more than a hundred and

sixty years and has always been quick to adapt to contemporary tastes, while remaining particularly famed for its bold embossed designs. Since 1972, the firm has been associated with names including Ulf Moritz, Jean Tinguely, Ludwig Mies van der Rohe, Alvar Aalto, Niki de Saint-Phalle and Theo van Doesburg, and its recent output includes Ulf Moritz's opulent metallic designs (see above), Richard Anuszkiewicz's Op art motifs, Karim Rashid's simple and sensual psychedelic motifs and Werner Berges's Pop art patterns, inspired by Andy Warhol.

The US and Canada

The Americans came relatively late to wallpaper manufacture, their enthusiasm fired by the French panoramic papers created by Zuber and Dufour. Brunschwig & Fils is a magnificent example of a successful US-based firm that has become established worldwide, recently launching a sublime collection of small-pattern wallpapers – in opposition to contemporary trends but quite possibly anticipating future ones.

Another great American brand, Wallquest, has a particularly interesting history, being linked to the Lafoys, a French family from Lyon who had began manufacturing wallpaper in 1820 and founded the firm Inaltera. In 1976, Inaltera opened an US branch, which was hugely successful, with clients including the White House and a great many celebrities. In 1985, the firm changed hands and changed names. Wallquest, as it was now known, continued to import wallpaper from France and then, in 1994, started producing paper in Pennsylvania. Once more a family-run firm, it sells high-quality wallpapers in a classic style, adapting traditional designs to suit contemporary tastes, and exporting worldwide.

German firm Marburg encourages contributions from artists and designers. Ulf Moritz's hi-tech designs from the Compendium *(opposite) and* Scala *collections (above) include hammered metallic effects, drop shapes made from silica sand, and a combination of handprinted, screenprinted and digital images.*

From left to right: *'Egrets' by Florence Broadhurst, from Signature Prints; 'Ming' by Pierre Frey; checked paper by Colefax and Fowler and a bag made from 'Uppark' by Farrow & Ball; 'Aquarius' by Pierre Frey.*

Left: *An interior by Barbara Becker for Rasch.*
Overleaf: *Sandberg find inspiration from history to create unmistakably contemporary wallpapers, such as this witty grisaille design, called 'Mr and Mrs Collins'.*

sual living   CLAIRE LLOYD

LA COULEUR DANS LA DÉCORATION

Kockaihös kokbok

The Canadians refuse to be left behind and are also producing sophisticated wallpapers: the Umbra brand, for example, sell a wide range of quality wallpapers around the globe.

Scandinavia

The Scandinavians were among the leading wallpaper manufacturers between the 1960s and the 1980s, bringing a new spirit of freedom to the field. Based in Sweden, Sandberg (see left and page 123) remains one of the most renowned brands, inspired by world travel and by grand old houses, creating beautiful Gustavian stripes and *trompe l'oeil* effects in soft pastel shades. Another prominent Swedish firm, BoråsTapeter, founded by Waldemar Andrén in 1905, bridges the gap between past and present by reissuing designs by Josef Frank and also offering customized digitally printed wallpapers via its Mr Perswall website.

Italy

The Italians were slow to embrace wallpaper, but have caught up with the rest of the world thanks to a handful of extremely beautiful brands. Montecolino, for example, was founded in the early 1970s and began producing floorings and textiles before turning to wallpaper with luxurious and avant-garde designs such as those of German designer Lars Contzen.

Zambaiti also started out as a family concern, when Angelo Zambaiti and his wife Angela began selling paper in Cagliari in 1936. Forty years and four sons later, Zambaiti launched its own brand and became the industry leader in Italy. Zambaiti also owns the Tiffanie brand, first set up in 1972 by Pickhardt & Siebert International, a German manufacturer which joined the Italian group in 1997 and began distributing its wallpapers in France. This brand produces a wide range of high-quality vinyl wallcoverings, printed on a particularly heavy paper (up to 500g/m²), which gives the products an exceptionally durable finish.

Jannelli & Volpi are also keeping up with the competition. The last three collections from their latest line, J&V Italian Design, have been classic and elegant, evoking Renaissance damasks, sophisticated eastern-inspired motifs and stylized florals, all top of the range.

Russia and East Asia

Japan was relatively slow to adopt the fashion for wallpaper, which it continues to import from the

West and which remains an expensive product reserved for an elite handful of customers as well as hotels and luxury stores. Korea has now begun producing its own wallpaper. China produces copies, to the point that many European manufacturers have been afraid to try and break into the Chinese market in case they provide their Chinese rivals with too much inspiration. Nonetheless, a handful of young designers have ventured to open showrooms in Shanghai displaying European-style wallpapers, although some now complain of being copied themselves.

All eyes now are on Russia, a country that is crazy about wallpaper and demands larger-than-usual widths (the norm there is 1.06 metres), opulent materials, lavish patterns, flocks, striking colours, and vibrant gold and silver: the kind of decor fit for a tsar. European manufacturers have been quick to grasp this new market. German firms have started to build state-of-the-art factories in Russia and the French now export their non-woven ranges to the Russian market – a market with a voracious appetite, buying up a hundred million rolls of wallpaper a year, which is as much as Britain and France put together.

From left to right: *Japanese Floral', 'Cockatoos' and 'Circles and Squares', sumptuous designs in bold colours by Florence Broadhurst, now reissued by Signature Prints, the Australian firm founded by Helen and David Lennie.*

Miss Broadhurst's extraordinary tale

Florence Broadhurst was a talented and eccentric Australian, born in rural Queensland in 1899. She travelled extensively and founded an academy of modern arts in the bustling city of Shanghai, then eventually opened a wallpaper company in her native Australia, using her own designs. A flamboyant designer and bold colourist who favoured combinations of fuchsia pink, lemon yellow, lime green, bright orange, turquoise, black, silver and gold, Broadhurst kept working until her death in 1977, at the age of seventy-eight, and her company, which was revolutionary for its day, monopolized the Australian market up until the mid-1970s, exporting wallpapers to as far afield as the US, Peru, France, the Middle East and Norway.

Florence Broadhurst's work has now been revived, thanks to the efforts of two enthusiasts, David and Helen Lennie. Their Sydney-based company, Signature Prints, specializes in the design and manufacture of luxury wallpapers using traditional screenprinting techniques, and have turned Florence Broadhurst's extraordinary design archive into a sumptuous range of papers (see right). Originally working on a small scale as little more than a niche business, Signature Prints have rapidly acquired an international reputation.

A New

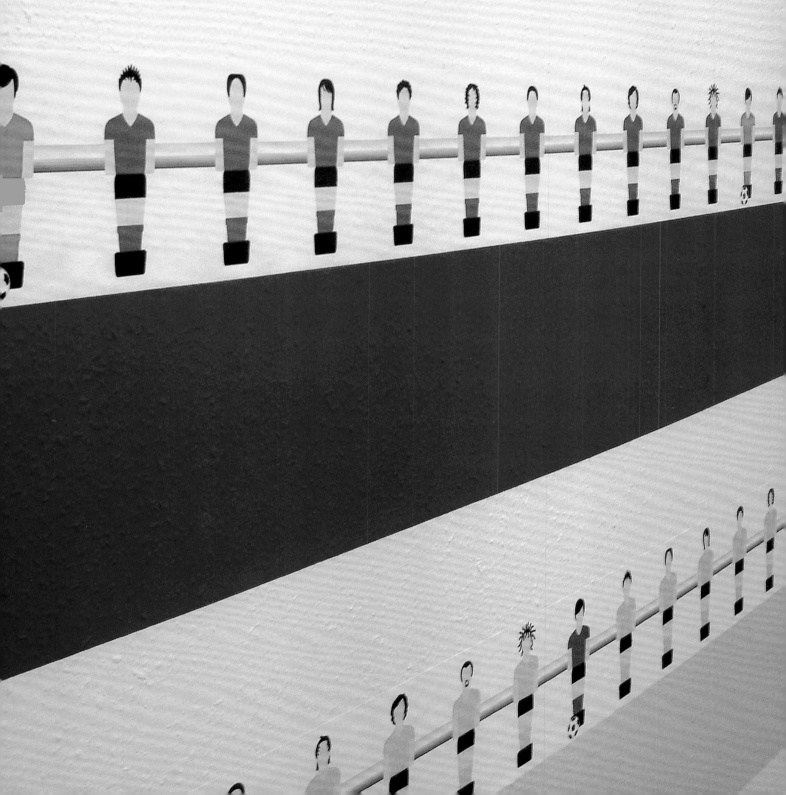

Wave

*T*he rules have changed, and now a new generation of designers are considering the countless possibilities that wallpaper has to offer. They are the children of the recession, Generation Y, at home with Twitter and iPads, and they are not interested in boundaries or conventions. Their only limits are the limits of photography, fashion, and digital design. Reconciled with the past, they are already flying headlong into the future, and to these multifaceted artists, wallpaper is simply another medium to be explored.

These designers are bold, energetically, jubilantly combining disciplines, embracing technology, reinventing patterns. In their hands, wallpaper does more than simply line a room: it forms a feature in itself. We've divided this new wave of designs into seven different themes, all of which are guaranteed to inspire a host of new ideas for your home.

Modern wallpaper is often used on a single feature wall to make a striking statement.
Opposite: *'Caviar', an exuberant and colourful design by German design house GoHome.*
Previous pages: *'Border Playboys' by Single-Tapete.*

Traditional with a twist

These designs reinterpret the styles of the early 19th century and retain a warm, familiar ambiance. Flowers, stripes and arabesque patterns are the basic ingredients, but with a touch of pizzazz to bring them up to date.

English designer Jane Churchill's wallpapers and matching fabrics aim to evoke both tranquillity and luxury. Her delicate stripes and subtle flowers are fresh and pleasing, and her children's ranges are inspired by Beatrix Potter and by Cicely Mary Barker's *Flower Fairies*, among others (see right).

Sandberg wallpapers are inspired by foreign travel and grand old houses. This Swedish brand's products are meticulously crafted, always hand-finished in an integrated studio to produce very delicate designs, and their beautiful broad stripes, muted shades, *trompe l'oeil* effects and stylized flowers (pages 125, 142–143) lend themselves particularly well to elegant interiors.

London-based designer Jocelyn Warner (see pages 118, 152) draws her inspiration from the natural world as well as from the 1950s, using a discreet range of colours but also seizing the opportunities offered by digital technology to push her graphic experiments towards larger formats and more sophisticated styling. Her florals, damasks and abstract motifs are based on a palette of neutral shades, greys, whites, jades and bronzes, while her use of iridescent and glossy inks to create a metallic look gives these classic designs a modern feel.

Anthropologie is a US brand who now own stores in the UK, and their wallpapers are more sophisticated than they may seem at first. The designs look deceptively peaceful and even childlike, but on closer inspection, rabbits and butterflies can be seen frolicking among thorny rose bushes where snakes lurk, shells and jewels grow on trees, jellyfish float through octopus gardens, and a design of traditional china plates is embellished with turtles, snails and buzzing beehives. Many of these designs are screenprinted, gilded or flocked, adding a luxurious touch.

Right: *Jane Churchill's designs typically include coordinating wallpaper and textiles and take their inspiration from childhood.*

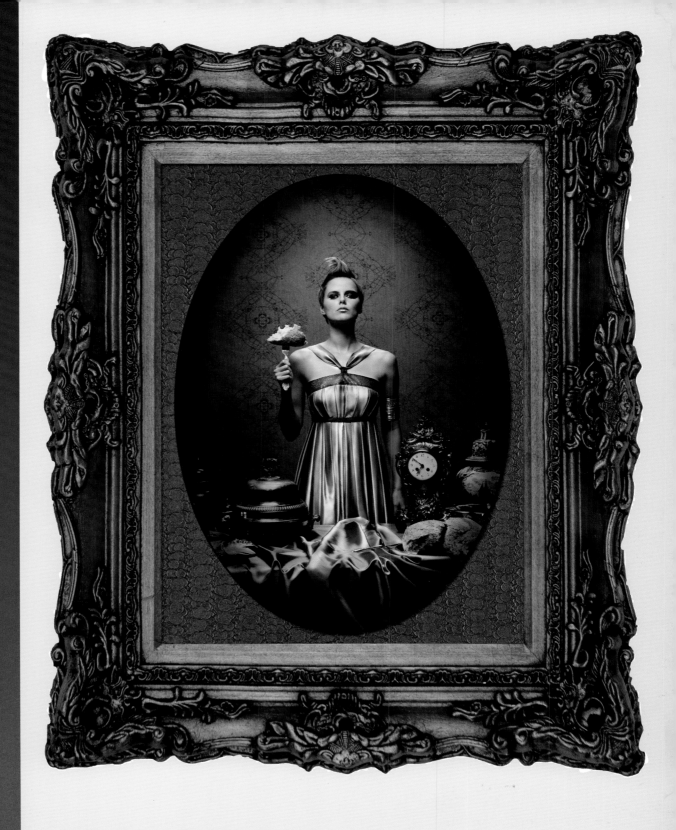

Hooked on glamour

The work of Hookedonwalls is an invitation into a deeply idiosyncratic world where the peculiar, poetic quality of the wallpapers is matched by design names such as 'Belgian Graffiti' and 'Jealous Walls'. 'Forget safe. Stand out,' the studio insists. Forget about safe prints, dull colours and boring paper. Hookedonwalls wallpaper is a daring statement, designed for those who are prepared to take risks. In the hands of these inspired Belgian designers, traditional patterns become sexy, damasks turn shabby chic and florals are lush and venomous. Even their catalogue borders on eccentricity: 'Liquid Fantasy' is displayed in a blurry underwater world, while 'Hysterical Glamour' features mysterious femmes fatales lounging in the lobby of a hotel, preparing for a masquerade. These creations are ideal for classic but quirky interiors, and for those who want to make a real statement.

Above: *'Glorious Revolution' by Hookedonwalls, a typical combination of eccentricity and glamour.*
Opposite: *'Leaf' by Jocelyn Warner, a London designer who favours textile effects and a subtle palette.*

Baroque revival

The new baroque is a reworking of the classical style, taking traditional damasks and animal motifs and playfully pushing them to their limits. The design duo Munchausen, formed in 2004 by Simon Pillard and Philippe Rossetti, are excellent representatives of this trend. Their strong graphics are highlighted by a deliberately restrained colour palette, mostly two-tone and often black and white, occasionally enlivened with a splash of something brighter. Munchausen combine tradition, literature and pop culture into a joyful mix of art and fun that is typical of the new generation of designers. In collaboration with fashion label Commune de Paris 1871, the duo reworked 19th-century engravings to create wallpaper, posters and T-shirts. For Ugly Edition, they designed a collection made up of giant-sized motifs – a damask pattern, orchids with blood-red throats, curious parrots (opposite) – that gave a dreamlike twist to classic subjects. 'Clouds', a particularly intriguing motif, won a special jury prize at the 'WallpaperLab' exhibition held at the Musée des Arts Décoratifs in Paris in 2006.

Two fantastical designs by Munchausen for Saint Honoré Wallcoverings.
Above: *'Bouquet'.*
Opposite: *'Parrots'.*

Scottish surrealism

The founders of the Glasgow design studio Timorous Beasties, Paul Simmons and Alistair McAuley, define their style as 'William Morris on acid'. This strange and talented duo produce wallpapers that are a blend of contemporary graphics, cutting-edge technology and old-world imagery. Their work is strange and provocative: their roses have thorns, their orchids are intertwined with sexually explicit manga imagery (page 237), their bees and butterflies are entomologically accurate (page 224), and a damask design is haunted by shadows of lost paintings, like evocative ghosts. They have also slipped scenes of grim reality into a superficially traditional toile de Jouy, which on closer inspection reveals a dilapidated urban landscape peopled with prostitutes and vagrants — a piece of thinly disguised social and political critique on the part of this committed duo, following closely in the footsteps of their compatriot Charles Rennie Mackintosh. The devil is in the detail, they believe, and their wallpapers in pearly white, gold, silver and black are both sumptuous and beautiful — but with a lethal twist.

When size is everything

The trend towards oversized motifs is a way of cocking a snook at convention and of dragging wallpaper to the forefront of decorative attention. Today's designers dare to think big, very big, whether that means full-blown rhododendrons, *toile de Jouy* monuments, 1970s-style geometrics or Art Deco extravagances. Used sparingly, often to create a statement wall, a single huge motif can become a work of art in its own right.

Markus Benesch utilizes larger-than-life motifs in his designs for Rasch and Jannelli & Volpi, sometimes in colour – as in his Op art and *trompe l'oeil* designs and his brilliant, intertwined ribbons dancing all over the wall – and sometimes relying exclusively on white-on-white, but always with a preference for the oversized.

Wall & Decò is an Italian company whose designers also specialize in large motifs. Using a mixture of photography and digital graphics, they create supersize close-ups, drawing their inspiration from Japanese and Arabic decorative art, pop culture, contemporary urban life and stylized elements of the natural world. Fairytale

orchids and gigantic koi carp by Giò Pagani, Herculean fingerprints, enormous poppies, a fencelike row of coloured pencils, pink flamingos higher than a door. These witty visuals are printed on a special vinyl that is fireproof and washable, making them both daring and practical.

The Dutch company Eijffinger, well known for its bespoke wallcoverings, is also a promoter of supersize style. Its *Wallpower Unlimited* collection features dramatically enlarged motifs in lace, cashmere and damask – as if a giantess had entered the house and left a scarf draped casually over a wall. In Germany, Bettina Gerlach's designs for Endless Wallpaper (see opposite) reflect a life lived on a large scale, with beetles crawling over stylized leaves, an oversized houndstooth check, huge branches of coral growing under water, and a swarm of life-size flies. The strong colours and expressive lines of her collection create a strangely sensual feel.

Unlike traditional designs, this type of wallpaper is not sold in rolls but in panels that are designed to be matched up horizontally, giving the motif space to stretch out, rather like a panorama.

Left: *'Hick's Hexagon' by David Hicks for Cole & Son.*
Opposite: *A Bettina Gerlach design for Endless Wallpapers; a quirky panoramic paper in which dreamlike elements float over an oversized houndstooth check.*

A German sense of humour

German brand GoHome Urban Wallpaper pushes the trend for outsize motifs to its limit. 'There are always moments in life when it's better to stay at home — no matter if it's because it's a rainy day or if the night before lasted a bit too long': this is the basic concept behind GoHome, where the aim is to create wallpaper that provides an incentive to stay at home, wallpaper that is as spectacular as it is cosy. Supersized motifs, vibrant colours and an element of wit serve as a starting point for each of its impressive creations. 'The Wheel', for example, is based on a fairground Ferris wheel; 'Octopus Pop' (above) was inspired by Bologna's fish market, and 'Caviar' (page 149) is straight from the counter of a New York deli, while the damask-like motif of 'Anakreon' (page 108) is inspired by the Greek poet of the same name, famed for his love of wine and women. GoHome's hybrid style is modern, personal and humorous, with just a touch of nostalgia.

Above: GoHome encapsulates contemporary urban trends with its oversized motifs and offbeat concepts. This design, 'Octopus Pop', was inspired by a trip to Italy.
Opposite: Since the 1950s, Finnish firm Marimekko has led the way with its simple but iconic motifs.

Time to play

The designs in this section are bright appealing and often inspired by the world of childhood. One example is the work of Absolute Zero°, the design studio founded by Londoners Mark Hampshire and Keith Stephenson, whose first wallpaper collection in 2004 was an immediate success. The delicate graphics of their seasonal range – 'Swallows', 'Bees' and 'Dandelions', for autumn, spring and summer, respectively – set a tone for their work, reflecting a nostalgic charm that refuses to take itself too seriously. Their *Playtime* collection is named after the Jacques Tati movie and a British brand of biscuits iced with the shapes of animals and toys, while the 'Knock Knock' design (see overleaf) is inspired by house door numbers. These simple motifs, rooted in everyday life, are given sophistication by their graphic lines, while the delicate colour palette makes the quirky designs surprisingly easy to live with.

A number of female designers are also creating original designs in a similarly playful style. Ulrika Gyllstad and Wilhelmina Wiese are the driving forces behind the Swedish company Bantie, whose witty designs, including a cute Japanese-inspired motif called 'Kokeshi' (page 235), can be combined with coordinated textiles to create a total look.

Spanish sensations

Spanish wallpapers reflect a light-hearted approach to life that is utterly infectious. Barcelona designer Ana Montiel refuses to take herself too seriously and has created a pretty geometric design called 'Topo' that she has used on everything from wallpaper to clothes for pets! Notwithstanding this lighthearted approach, the paper is handprinted and available in a sumptuous matt gold version as well as shades of blue and brown.

The company Coordonné was founded in 1978 and remains at the cutting edge of Spanish design. collaborating regularly with artists and preferring small collections that have a strong brand look. The *Vital* collection by illustrator Jordi Labanda (pages 100–101, 164–165) incorporates his trademark stylized female figures and continues to be one of the firm's bestsellers, while Coordonné's unusual children's collection invites us into a world of fantasy and adventure that is never twee.

Tres Tintas are also based in Barcelona, and also associated with designs that are fresh, youthful and modern. In 2004, three brothers, sons of the founder of the famous Aribau wallpaper store, decided to carry on the family tradition and began by reissuing a range of European designs from the 1960s and 1970s, first sold by their father, but given a striking new colour palette and the collection name *Revival*. More designer collections followed, all stylish, elegant and fun. One such series, *9 Selvas de Mariscal*, is the creation of acclaimed graphic designer Javier Mariscal, while another, *Wall-à-Porter*, is inspired by the world of women's fashion. More recently, the three brothers have launched a collection that pays homage to the home of Sophie von Fürstenberg. An indefatigable traveller and inspired photographer, this eccentric German aristocrat transformed her apartment in the historic centre of Barcelona into a vibrant retreat where she could recover from her

A human touch

Andrew Hardiman is a young designer who has succeeded in carving a niche for himself in the hectic world of British design thanks to his enchanting wallpaper range, Kuboaa. Taking his inspiration from nature and everyday objects, he has created an idiosyncratic and highly personal collection, featuring oversized florals alongside bold geometric motifs, pearl finishes and a bright acid palette. The two-colour repeat motifs often include witty touches, such the stags that peer through a pattern of sequoia branches, or a mass of tropical leaves crisscrossed by a trellis of escalators, carrying tiny commuters through the jungle.

Above and opposite: *'Pet Sounds' and 'Knock Knock', two witty designs by London duo Absolute Zero°.* **Overleaf:** *'Mots mêlés' (background), a wordsearch wallpaper, and 'Morpion' (inset), a noughts-and-crosses design, both by 5.5 Designers for Lutèce .*

Games without frontiers

The four members of French studio 5.5 Designers aim to decompartmentalize the design process by creating links between an object and its user. Combining traditional forms with playful innovations is one way of achieving this. By applying their ideas to wallpaper — as a new medium of expression — they have produced witty designs that are full of the unexpected. The papers in their **Wallpaper Games** range are covered with wordsearches, mazes or games of noughts and crosses, inviting viewers to play an active and creative role, and have proved a great commercial success. This is a truly interactive wallpaper that allows people to give free reign to their imaginations by changing what is on their walls from day to day with a marker pen.

```
MPENSATO                HAALOG
ATORNETMNTSLMHAA   EMEHDMAIAIETUU
AIUDCNNIENSLEELEM    ANCBRLEYQUITTE
TEAYIEFNOUIILBEUIANC   ASEORSURGELE
HGUMAUSOANFTABASEARLA    LPNIMEHCRA
ENDREUCAUCHEMARSVREAEHLPNIMEHCRA ZAGRA
CAMOTEREGRUBMAH ARMISTICE LLEZAGRA
BEFFACEURIOLUOVMEEM ALABAR ISEENAC
ULTIMATUMCOURSIER MOBYLETTE EUGOGA
RECIDIVISTES URDIMENSIONNEFRITEON
MBRELCATIBAHDFONPONTEALPAL PARTI
EREDIMARYPRIAUAOAHNENTEAINEAEEB
COEOMNIVOREVSURILOYIIRICTSELNMC
OUESEHTNYSOTOHPSMUEPLBAMUNAIOTAU
NULTIMBRERERNATETRSIOREOROFINILTUHI
NOBEURSAANTEAEIEPLEVDGFRO LOUVET
AIHAUCEBBXEMTUNCEGIANRLICCMEQDR
IQDPAQLMUOBIEIROEVDUMRARTYTIRANID
SEULOEOEUOAERITOROEORGMA ENCAMERAE
SSEEMCNCUNHBETOBCMLETNSALSEPAREI
AMIERNNRAOPIIOCEEGFIILAMIIMEDCC
BCNEOEIAELLMTAHBICTJOCOBAUSIIHS
LTKCRN ACRE APIHPRLIBALARAUH TELU
ESPHYNX UPFNRUCOMIRCUSOGERMCACATO
OUX MINORITAIRE PLUOOTLRUGNOREITELEP
OCOREILLON SMFFGLIASHMRNOREEN RUES
GEIRIODIAL PLAGE MIRQRAEREENOITUTI
VTEAVIS ALADNAMAREDUOCCOTON BRONCHI
UCHONTOL SALADNA ACUITE MEDINDIRECTERIOHC
LETONEIUOHCEMEDIPELETTETNEMELASO
TARITHMETIQUEPIPELETTERAVIVE
ERNELETSUOGNALFACILITERAVIVE
RICULTURETCOEEEREMERTUO SENTEN
LORECNDHNART CAM
RDCAORAERTOALOEI
```

adventures, develop her negatives and host her artistic soirées. This fabulous space, decorated with mosaics, once welcomed guests including Gaudí, Picasso and Dalí. Now it has inspired the motifs and the textures of the Tres Tintas *Sophie* collection, which in turn reflect some of the mystery and sophistication of this charismatic woman.

The king of illusions

The Koziel brand is named after its creator, Christophe Koziel, who gave up his job in advertising in 2005 at the age of thirty-three to pursue a career in wallpaper design. His world of contemporary *trompe l'oeil* designs is relaxed and uninhibited with a strongly artistic streak that produces wonderfully dramatic interiors, playfully manipulating our senses to create frissons of surprise and fun. The Koziel wallpaper range includes antique wood panelling, trophies that look more real than the real thing, and a false brick wall. 'Byblio' simulates a set of shelves packed with leather-bound books, while 'Kapyton' recreates the look of hand-padded leather, creating a real sense of volume, light and texture. On the lighter side, 'ToiletSpirit' (see opposite) features rolls of pink toilet paper stacked from floor to ceiling, the sense of depth enhanced by its slightly spongy texture. It's sure to bring an unusual touch to life's inevitable moments of solitude.

Opposite, above:
'Kaleidoscope', a spectacular design by Jordi Labanda for the Spanish firm Coordonné.
Opposite, below right:
'ToiletSpirit', a trompe l'oeil *paper by Koziel.*
Overleaf, left: *'Fog'* by Antoine + Manuel.
Overleaf, right: *'Christine K.'* by Single-Tapete.

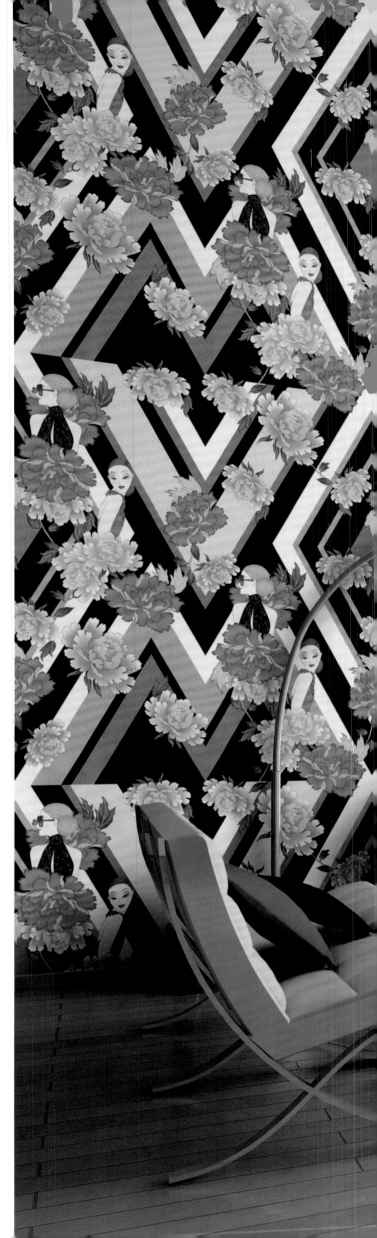

Creativity through competition

As much a research laboratory as an observatory of current trends, the WallpaperLab competition arose from a partnership between A3P, the French association for the promotion of wallpaper, and the Musée des Arts Décoratifs in Paris. Thanks to the work of Véronique de la Hougue, curator of the museum's wallpaper department, WallpaperLab serves as a channel of communication between the industry and designers, two worlds that are both opposite and complementary, and brings them together to promote innovative design for tomorrow's walls. Every two years, in the autumn, a selection of entries is examined by a jury of experts, then exhibited in the museum the following summer. So far, the competition has uncovered talents as diverse as Antoine + Manuel (see below) and Philippe Model. In 2010, the WallpaperLab prize was awarded to Jean–Louis Fréchin and Uros Petrevski of Nodesign.net, for their 'augmented' wallpaper embedded with digital information that can be revealed by a means of an iPhone app, overlaying everyday decor with a ghostlike world of memories.

Graphic opulence

French design studio Antoine + Manuel is run by Antoine Audiau and Manuel Warosz, who began collaborating in 1993. The duo work mainly in the spheres of culture and fashion, producing fresh interpretations of a familiar visual world and deploying this opulent graphic language in their wallpapers. For example, 'Fog' (this page) is complex and bold: a greyscale landscape that incorporates brightly coloured architectural elements.

Free and single

German interior designers Susanne Schmidt and Andrea Baum have created a range of 'wallpaper for single people', which won the special jury prize at the first New Walls, Please! competition in Frankfurt. Now sold under the brand name Single–Tapete, motifs like the one on this page are designed to be perfect housemates for urban singletons: friendly, fun and easy to live with, but never dull.

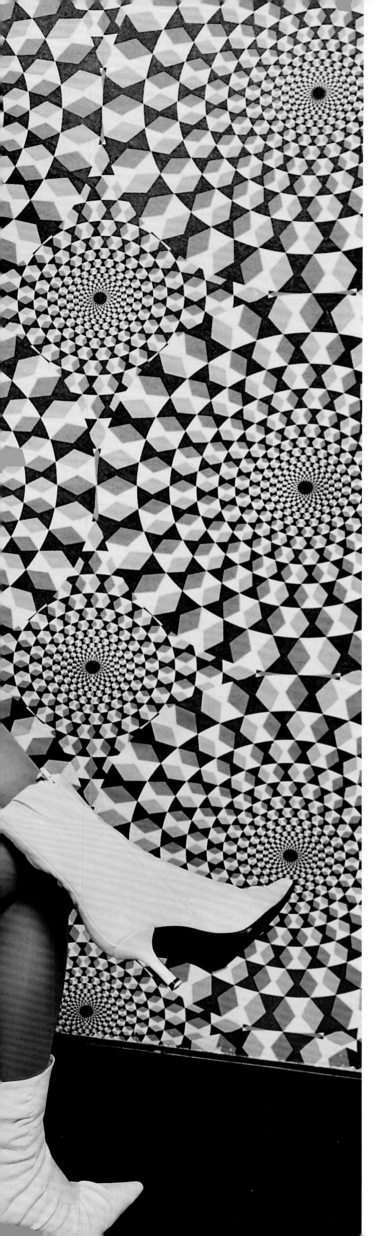

Retro style

Was it the Spanish design trio Tres Tintas who first started the retro wallpaper craze with their *Revival* collection in 2004? Whoever it was, the fashion for anything retro – the mod styles of the fifties, the flower power of the sixties, the disco chic of the seventies – has spread like wildfire over the last decade. Designers have applied their imagination to reviving and reinterpreting a weath of striking post-war styles, and now many major brands, including Graham & Brown, Osborne & Little, and Cole & Son in the UK, and A.S. Création in Germany, have incorporated retro motifs and unashamedly kitsch designs into their collections. Textile designer Teija Bruhn created the *OAS* range for Swedish firm Decor Maison, incorporating stylized flowers, psychedelic leaves and bold stripes in a range of beiges, reds and browns. To echo the nostalgic theme, Decor Maison even used caravans to showcase the designs in its catalogue (see page 170). Another Swedish manufacturer, Svenskt Tenn, has reissued several beautiful floral designs that date back to the 1940s.

In Germany, Tapeten der 70er ('Wallpaper from the 70s') specializes in reissuing wallpapers with kaleidoscopic retro graphics, all of which can be ordered online. Whether surrealist, abstract or glamorous, their wallpapers come in a startling range of colours and are an irresistible invitation to step back in time. Another German, the designer Lars Contzen, has created a collection of non-woven vinyls in a bold graphic style (see overleaf), with a carefully chosen colour range that gives a new lease of life to florals, damasks and geometric prints. And finally, Berlintapete, which sells print-on-demand digital wallpapers and photo murals online, includes an impressive selection of stunning retro motifs in its catalogue.

Left: *'Veruso Illusion', a retro design from German vintage specialists Tapeten der 70er.*

A taste of yesterday

Lovers of genuine vintage wallpaper can source it from specialist internet suppliers. Auctions and the closure of shops and factories feed the supply and hundreds of rolls of original papers are available for purchase online and are posted out in their original packaging, carrying with them a distinctive whiff of the past. E.W. Moore in the UK, Secondhand Rose in the US, and FunkyWalls in Belgium are just a few of these treasure troves of vintage style.

Above: *A nostalgic showcase for a design from the OAS collection, designed for the Swedish brand Decor Maison by Teija Bruhn.*
Opposite: *'Light Circles' by German designer Lars Contzen, who is inspired by 1960s graphics.*

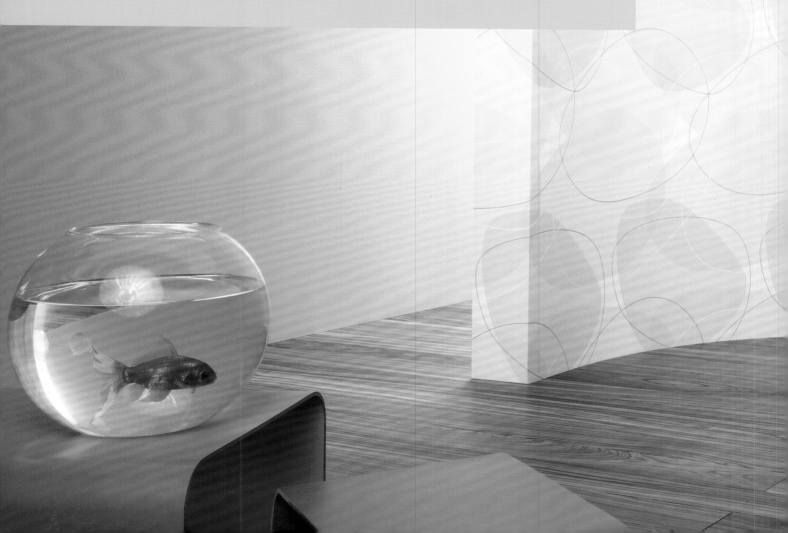

Technopapers

In the 20th century, the great wallpaper revolution was the advent of papers that were non-woven, longlasting, easy to hang and equally easy to strip. The technology of the 21st century is already bringing designers exciting new opportunities to bring the walls of our homes to life, with wallpapers that are phosphorescent, light-emitting, scented, magnetic, heat-sensitive or even digitally interactive.

French firm Moove-Paper have created a product that allows users to change their wallpaper whenever they feel like it. First, a row of self-adhesive magnetic strips are attached to the wall, then the made-to-measure design is printed on metallic paper that can be easily affixed to the magnets and just as easily removed when you decide on a change of scene. The Moove-Paper catalogue offers a wealth of designs that can be used for this game of 'musical walls', including images from the Roger-Viollet picture archives. The *Musées & Co* range, created in association with France's national museums, enables customers to own a king-size work of art (see right), while a collection by Parisian designer Philippe Model offers lifesized *trompe l'oeil* photographs of his interior designs.

Scientists in the US and Japan have already begun to design wallpaper that incorporates solar cells, exploiting the sustainable power source of sunlight. The latest technology allows the cells to be printed directly onto paper, keeping manufacturing

Above left: *Gustave Caillebotte's painting* The Floor Scrapers *(1875), transformed into magnetic moveable wallpaper by Moove-Paper.*
Below left: *'First Look' from the Senses collection by Muurbloem, a Dutch design studio.*

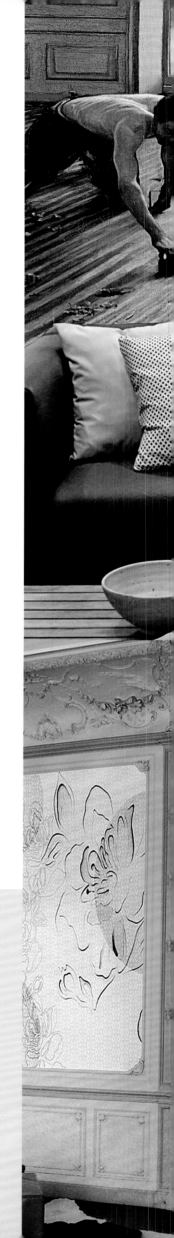

Natural beauties

A German of Italian origin, based in Switzerland, designer Luigi Colani has made human beings and their interaction with their environment the focus of his work. His forms are inspired by the perfection of nature, as evidenced by his amazing collection of wallpapers for Marburg, based on the idea that water is the source of all life. The motifs represent water in all its states — from tiny droplets to breaking waves, from opaque surfaces to shimmering transparency. Thanks to sophisticated printing technology, the designs change colour according to the angle from which they are viewed, and the rather masculine palette is enhanced by lustre and iridescence, a subtle interweaving of matt and gloss effects, like sunlight glittering on water. This magical collection can be further enhanced by the addition of decorative metal 'drops' that can be affixed to the paper.

Freeze frame

The advent of digital imaging has allowed photography
to create a new niche for itself in the world of wallpaper.
Ultra-large photographs can now be turned into wall
decorations, bridging the gap between art and mass
production. Like yesterday's painters, today's photographers
are now discovering the possibilities of wallpaper design.

Alain Balter and Didier Cocatrix, who work under the
name Co-Balt, have an extensive photo library, particularly
of architectural images, while Valérie Monthuit, a keen
observer of nature, specializes in minutely detailed close-ups,
in which the microcosm of nature turns into an enchanting
dreamworld. Based in Portugal, For-Arte, founded by Pedro
Pereira, offers customized designs based on artists' works and
contemporary photographs and has an image bank of more
than six million images, which can be also be digitally coloured
to order. German brand Extratapete specializes in custom
panoramic papers made from photographic elements or digital
images, which are stripped their surrounding elements and
simplified to form bold motifs (pages 176–177).

Let there be light!
Above and left: *'Ecco Luce',
a paper that incorporates
LEDs by Dutch designer
Jonas Samson.*
Opposite: *Glow-in-the-dark
wallpaper by Cocobohème.*
Overleaf, above: *'Tokyo
Metro' (left) and 'Timbuktu'
(right) by Extratapete.*
Overleaf, below: *'Paris–
London' from the Fairy
Light range by Myrine
Créations.*

costs low. It is hoped that this solar-powered wallpaper, which generates enough electricity to power small appliances, will be available to the general public in the not-too-distant future.

Dreaming of a softer, calmer world, the innovative Belgian studio Buzzispace has invented the 'Buzziskin', an idiosyncratic and aesthetically pleasing wallpaper with sound-absorbent qualities. Available in self-adhesive rolls, it has a fuzzy texture and creates a cosy, warm ambiance. The French designers known as Cocobohème, Catherine Fouchard and Christian Mégevand, have come up with a glow-in-the-dark wallpaper (see above) that creates a different look by day and night, while Dutch designer Jonas Samson incorporates LEDs into his wallpaper (opposite).

At French studio Myrine Créations, Carole-My de Lépine and Perrine Beaujouan take an ultra-contemporary approach to wallcoverings, attempt to create a new generation of so-called 'intelligent' wallpapers by importing existing technology from other fields and applying it to wallpaper. Sold in panels, like paintings, its *Thermoactif* range incorporates heat-sensitive motifs that become visible or change colour when the temperature changes. The paper 'Sakumiji', for example, depicts a Japanese maple whose red leaves disappear in

the heat and are replaced by little pink flowers. The papers in the *Fairy Light* range, such as 'Paris–London' (overleaf, below), contain LEDs and are backed with an electrical panel that plugs into the mains: simply switch it on and the motif lights up. Another range, *UV*, is printed with inks that glow in ultraviolet light. Less high tech, but equally interactive, 'Remember Wall' is an all-over motif composed of messages written on coloured Post-it notes, a set of which are supplied with the wallpaper so that customers can personalize the paper with their own messages. Another design, 'Ventil'O', is decorated with miniature paper windmills that actually spin around.

Dutch design studio Muurbloem are also dedicated to exploring new sensations; the papers from the *Senses* collection (page 173, below) include 'Look', 'Sound', 'Taste', 'Feeling' and 'Smell' and are deliberately designed to trigger our perceptions.

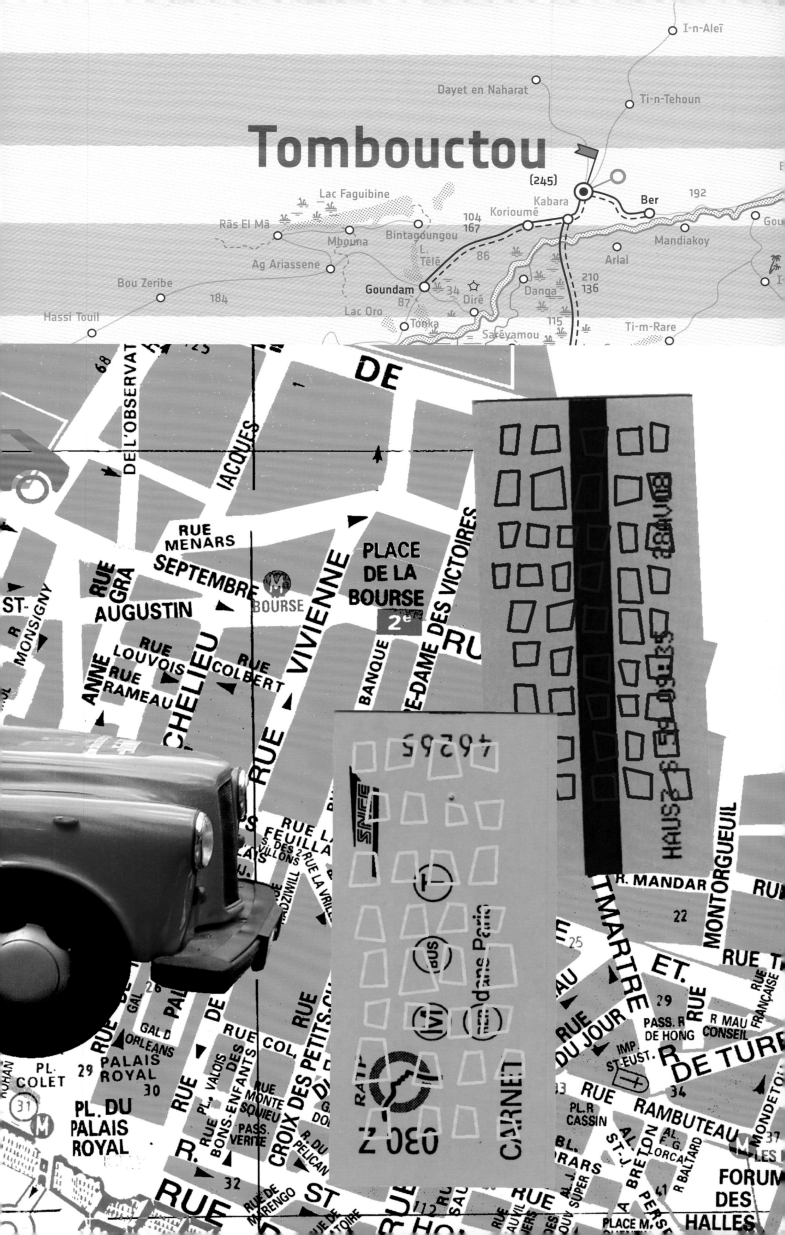

Artistic expressions

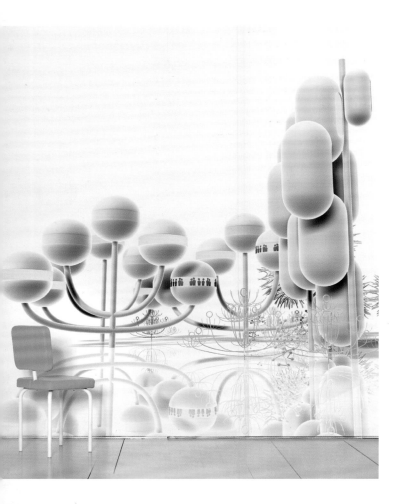

The advent of digital design does not mean that the hand of the artist is no longer required. Some manufacturers have chosen to collaborate with artists to create wallpapers with what we might call 'added value'. For example, René Kormann and his team at In Création in Paris have been building their range since 2004, favouring unusual motifs by textile designers, artists and architects, or drawn from the notebooks of great travellers. Every contributor has something unique to share: views of the Nile or Japan, street scenes, life drawings, *trompe l'oeil* images, *mises en abyme* and line art can used to open up walls, ceilings and closets, turning them into private dreamworlds. These original designs are often very bold: Mélanie Bénéfice's luscious vegetation (see opposite), Valérie B. Cartier's playful shower of confetti, Erol Gülgönen's sketched cityscape, Antoine Desailly's comical cockroaches, Pierre Alivon's colourful urban collages or the typographical experiments of font designer Albert Boton – all striking motifs that create unusual interiors.

For most designers exploring the potential of digital imaging, bespoke products are the supreme exercise in style. High-quality printing opens up all sorts of new imaginative territory, and the format allows for a bold approach: with panels that can measure as much as 11 metres long by 4.5 metres wide, anything is possible! Several stylish hotels, including the Hôtel Joyce and the Crown Plaza in Paris, and the Palacio Avenida in Palma de Mallorca, have taken advantage of this fact and commissioned designs from In Création.

Based in the Netherlands, Maxalot has been collaborating with artists who work exclusively in digital media since 2003. The company organizes exhibitions, takes part in art fairs and festivals, and has its own gallery in Amsterdam. Making use of the very latest in print technology, its *Exposif* wallpaper project incorporates designs by almost sixty international artists, bringing together a broad spectrum of graphic and design styles, with particularly strong links to illustration, graffiti and street art (see overleaf).

In France, Domestic, a firm run by Stéphane Arriubergé and Massimiliano Iorio, also works collaboratively with designers, graphic artists and artists, offering collections of objects that are inspired by unusual ideas and grouped thematically. In 2003, the duo launched their *Wall Drawings* range of wall stickers, which at the time were a new concept in the world of interior design, and their range of scenic wallpapers, launched in 2008, brought new life to a field that had been unfairly neglected since the 1980s. In the space of a year, some twenty designers, including Ich & Kar, have joined forces with the firm. The striking *Domestic by Colette* range, launched in 2007, has been followed by designs by Matali Crasset (see above), Jeremy Scott, Geneviève Gauckler, Antoine + Manuel (page 166), Hanna Werning, Jon Burgerman and Marcel Wanders (pages 134–135), among others.

A wall can become a limitless canvas for the imagination.
This page: 'O Tigre' (above) and 'O Hibou' (below) by Mélanie Bénéfice, one of the young designers working for In Création.
Opposite: 'D Fuse Landscape One', a scenic wallpaper by Matali Crasset for Domestic.

Since 2003, Dutch gallery Maxalot has promoted young artists who specialize in digital design. This wallpaper, 'Fuji One', is the work of French photographer and art director Pier Fichefeux.

Glowing with success

Before they turned their attention to wallpaper, Héléna Ichbiah and Piotr Karczewski — who work under the name Ich & Kar — were already well known for their original approach to graphic design, which was lyrical, cheeky and stripped down to basics rather than fussy or faddish. The success of their first range of wall stickers and the plethora of paler imitations that followed them encouraged Héléna and Piotr to turn their attention to wallpaper, and the result has been a range of simple but inspired flights of fancy. These whimsical creations, with their roots firmly anchored in reality, are perfectly at home anywhere.

First to come was a series featuring multiplication tables and French verb conjugations, nostalgically recalling the world of the classroom, followed by a design entitled 'Les Mots du lait', which used a complex typographical grid to display milk-related words, and finally 'Ocean', a charming map of the world composed only of oceans, seas and currents, a sort of liquid paradise. But the shining star of their collection has been their Phosphowall range, designed for the German company Rasch and printed with phosphorescent inks that make the motifs glow in the dark. Featuring bold, graphic flowers, stripes, swirling lines and black cats with green eyes (above and opposite), these papers lead a double life. They are ideal for stairwells and corridors: by day, the bright colours cheer up dull connecting spaces, and by night, there is no need to fumble in the dark for the light switch!

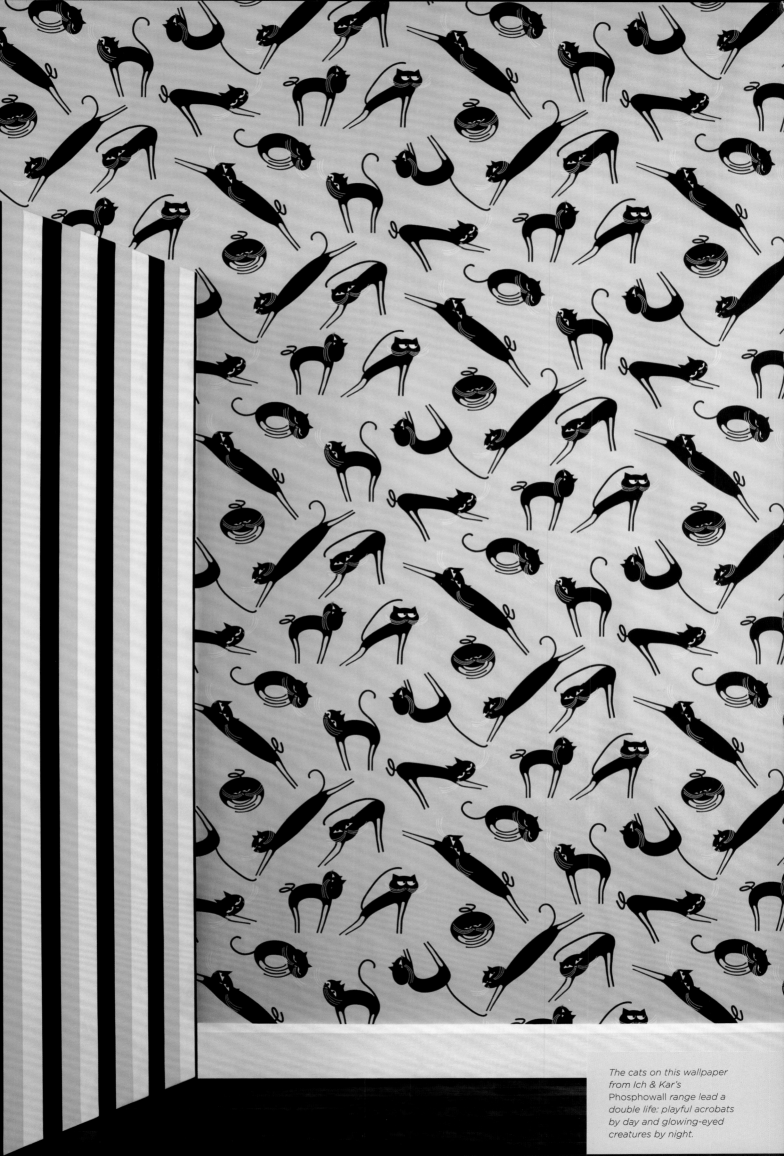

The cats on this wallpaper from Ich & Kar's Phosphowall *range lead a double life: playful acrobats by day and glowing-eyed creatures by night.*

Women's work

For a long time, wallpaper was an entirely male affair: the designers, engravers, printers and entrepreneurs involved were all men. The situation changed after the First World War, when women were propelled into the workplace and a handful of prominent female artists began projecting their ideas onto wallpaper. Since then, a great many women with a clearly defined creative agenda have followed suit. Among the pioneers were French textile designers Paule Marrot and Suzanne Fontan, whose motifs are characterized by lightness and purity, the Germans Margret Hildebrand and Elsbeth Kupferoth and the English designer Lucienne Day, all taking a stylish modernist approach, and Armi Ratia from Finland, the founder of Marimekko (see page 159). The delightfully engaging Zofia Rostad, a student of Paule Marrot, owes a debt to all of these women. Originally from Poland, Rostad has been one of France's best-known designers over the last thirty years, putting her name to some thirty collections for top manufacturers including Lutèce, Rasch, Essef and Vénilia. Her wallpapers use a distinctively bright colour palette, sometimes inspired by Polish folklore, and always treated with a light touch.

Staying spontaneous

Working with both textiles and wallpaper, Zofia Rostad regards fine art and decorative art as mutually inspiring and has always made light of technical constraints. 'When I'm starting out with a design,' she says, 'I work like a painter, while respecting the technical parameters of printing…. I have to keep the image in mind and make sure that size and colour restrictions don't limit my sense of artistic spontaneity.'

The new generation

Inspired by those early pioneers, a whole generation of young designers and illustrators have thrown themselves energetically into wallpaper design. They do much of the work by hand – painting, embroidering, sculpting, creating moments of sheer poetry. Polish designer Marta Budkiewicz has developed a style that is very free and intense, producing designs that are both precise and random. Her life-size silhouettes of people and furniture (see opposite) resemble sketchily drawn graffiti. German illustrator Birgit Amadori's fairytale creations, inspired by stories and legends from around the world, bring together east and west, enchanted forests, mysterious worlds, myths and dreamlike figures with huge originality, while the young American Aimée Wilder evokes a cool world of nostalgia (see below).

Rule Britannia

Across the Channel, the 1960s are associated with one name in particular – that of Laura Ashley, high priestess of traditional florals. Her stylistic heirs include Nina Campbell, who brings a fresh and charming approach to traditional themes, creating a world of butterflies, parrots and curious fish; Tricia Guild (page 190) with her unmistakable colour palette; the supremely inventive Tracy Kendall (overleaf), and Jocelyn Warner (pages 118, 152), who brings the natural world indoors, combining it with a restrained palette and metallic effects. All of them are inventive and original designers who combine lyricism with a touch of eccentricity. And today a great many other rising stars have snatched up the baton, including the ultra-chic Allegra Hicks, London designer Emily Todhunter, whose impeccable designs are inspired by the urban style of the 1940s and 1950s and the great British tradition of comfort chic, and Claire Coles, whose hand-embroidered wallpapers with their giant vintage-inspired motifs attain an ethereal beauty.

Erica Wakerly is inspired by the natural world and combines modern techniques and materials, while playing around with perspective in interesting ways. At design collective Custhom, Jemma Ooi specializes in floral and graphic papers with metallic foil details and heat-sensitive motifs. Scottish designer Johanna Basford transforms nature into a world of the imagination inhabited by superbly detailed flora and fauna, using special inks to create sophisticated matt, satin and pearlized effects that also feel wonderful to the touch. And, finally, the young Welsh designer Rebecca Ellen worked in textiles before making a name for herself with her printed and embroidered wallpapers. Her hugely original designs are inspired by mundane reality: landscapes, urban architecture and everyday objects transfigured into poetry, proving that, with talent, the ordinary can become extraordinary.

Left: *'Analognights' by the American designer Aimée Wilder.*
Opposite: *A sketched figure by Polish designer Marta Budkiewicz for The Collection.*

Tracy Kendall's wall art

It's hard to underestimate how new and different Tracy Kendall's wallpaper designs appeared in 2000, when the young designer began treating wallpaper almost like a textile, manipulating it, weaving it and producing 3D effects – one of the first designers to do so. 'I want them to convey a strong idea but not to dominate the room so much that there is no room for anything else,' she says of her designs (see right). Her motifs, simplified to the point where they become the purest expressions of reality, rarely go unnoticed, however, even when the motif is based on nothing fancier than a weed or a pigeon's feather lying on the pavement. Sewn-on sequins inspired by the glamorous fashions of the 1920s, a mosaic of fluttering words that send shadows dancing across the wall, paper fringes that ripple when touched, a jigsaw puzzle, thousands of buttons – Kendall's creations give walls a new sense of depth.

Magnified views of everyday objects are another of her favoured motifs. Piles of books or plates, cutlery, kitchen utensils, a single flower, or a giant feather can create a spectacular visual impact. But despite her many imitators, Kendall's designs remain distinctive, thanks to their pure lines and subtle colourways. 'In essence, wallpaper should be an enhancement to, and a confirmation of, the style and direction of an interior space,' says Kendall, adding: 'William Morris's statement "Have nothing in your houses that you do not know to be useful, or believe to be beautiful" is still as relevant today as a hundred years ago.'

Sewn-on buttons, oversized cutlery and fluttering pieces of paper are all the work of designer Tracy Kendall.

Right: *'Anichov Leaf' shows off Tricia Guild's distinctive colour palette of shocking pink, blue and green.*
Opposite: *Three creations by Louise Body: 'Harry's Garden' (top left), 'Holy Cow' (bottom left) and 'Erotica' (bottom right).*

Tricia Guild: variations on the theme of style

Back in 1970, when she first opened the Designers Guild boutique in London's King's Road, selling what amounted to an entire lifestyle, no one had heard of Tricia Guild. Unable to find the dream fabric she wanted for her own home, she recoloured an Indian blockprinted fabric instead, and Indian-inspired prints became the basis of her early success. Now, forty years later, the designer heads a small empire and launches two collections of coordinated wallpaper and fabric every year. The daring colours — shocking pink, turquoise and lime green — that surprised the world of interior design in 1970 have become Tricia Guild's trademark, and her talent lies in endlessly reinventing her palette and using it in designs that are striking but nonetheless blend harmoniously with other decor. Every new collections follows on seamlessly from the one before.

A keen traveller, the slim, raven-haired Guild never tires of overseeing the printing of her designs and of coming up with new ideas, often inspired by architectural landmarks such as Brighton's Royal Pavilion or the Palais Stoclet in Brussels. 'It's always changing for me,' she says. 'My collections are an expression of life; they are always moving. It's a bit like being an artist who has a language that's highly personal but never paints the same painting twice... Quality is fundamental. For me, every design is special. I'm very fussy about print quality and detail and the choice of paper and inks. It's these things that create the feel of a wallpaper, and that's particularly important... The colour matters as much as the pattern; a single shade can turn something subtle into something vulgar. Black, for instance, is never actually black. When I'm asked about choosing wallpaper, I always say: "Choose what resonates with you, and don't be afraid of big motifs. Strike a balance between wallpaper and plain finishes." An easy place to start is the entrance hall! You can try out something bold there. You have to be daring.'

The Body beautiful

'I have a bit of an obsession with birds,' admits Louise Body, renowned for her wallpapers covered with flocks of feathered friends. From a distance, her designs have a traditional look, but closer inspection reveals cheeky little details, such as tiny spiders clambering up the roses. One of Body's designs is named 'Harry's Garden' after an old family friend, another is based on her grandmother's pressed fern collection; another imitates a pair of old-fashioned lace curtains so convincingly that it is hard to tell it from the real thing. Her little birds twitter to each other on branches and flit around outside their cages, rejoicing in their freedom — just like the designer herself. She prints her wallpapers in very small runs, but it's easy to understand why when you learn that she coloured all three hundred birds on her 'Garden Birds' paper by hand. Her faded colours and old-world charm imbue a room with a gentle, romantic nostalgia.

The Collection includes wallpapers by many young European designers.
This page: *The three panels that make up 'Jungle' by Sophie Cordey.*
Opposite: *Two hand-embroidered trompe l'oeil papers by Aurélie Mathigot, 'Tour Eiffel' and 'Pois'.*

Talent spotting

When Allison Grant first turned up at the Maison et Objet trade fair in Paris, from England, in January 2003, with several rolls of wallpaper under her arm, the exhibitors were scornful and the organizers of the event promptly sent her away again. Wallpaper was out of style. But Grant did not believe it, and felt that walls were a huge area of untapped potential. To prove her point, she opened a shop in Paris called The Collection, selling designs by Tracy Kendall and Deborah Bowness, whose innovative treatment of the medium (exchanging the roll for the broad panel) opened up a host of new possibilities.

Allison Grant continues to sell designs from top international designers and studios including Makelike (US), Ilias Fotopoulos (Australia) and Camilla Diedrich (Sweden), while constantly keeping her eye open for new talent. The Collection also features stunning work from French and British designers, including Rebecca Ellen's embroidered wallpaper, witty designs by Lizzie Allen and Marta Budkiewicz's three-panel sketches (page 187), alongside work by Hélène Manche, Mayte Alcade and Émilie Rabiller. On the showroom walls, Jaime Salm's 3D panels and trompe l'oeil designs by Wallfurniture appear alongside friezes by Les Farfelus Farfadets and Danish designer Lene Toni Kjeld's unusual 'hybrid' papers, proving that wallpaper can become a work of art.

Grant's success is closely bound up with 'new wave' wallpaper, a movement that she has helped to build and continues to promote by scouring international trade shows in search of new gems. She also sells The Collection through a dedicated website, which includes delicate creations by Sophie Cordey (see above), as well as Aurélie Mathigot's dreamily nostalgic images (opposite) and the 3D modular designs of Mathilde Nivet. It seems that walls still contain a lot of room to explore.

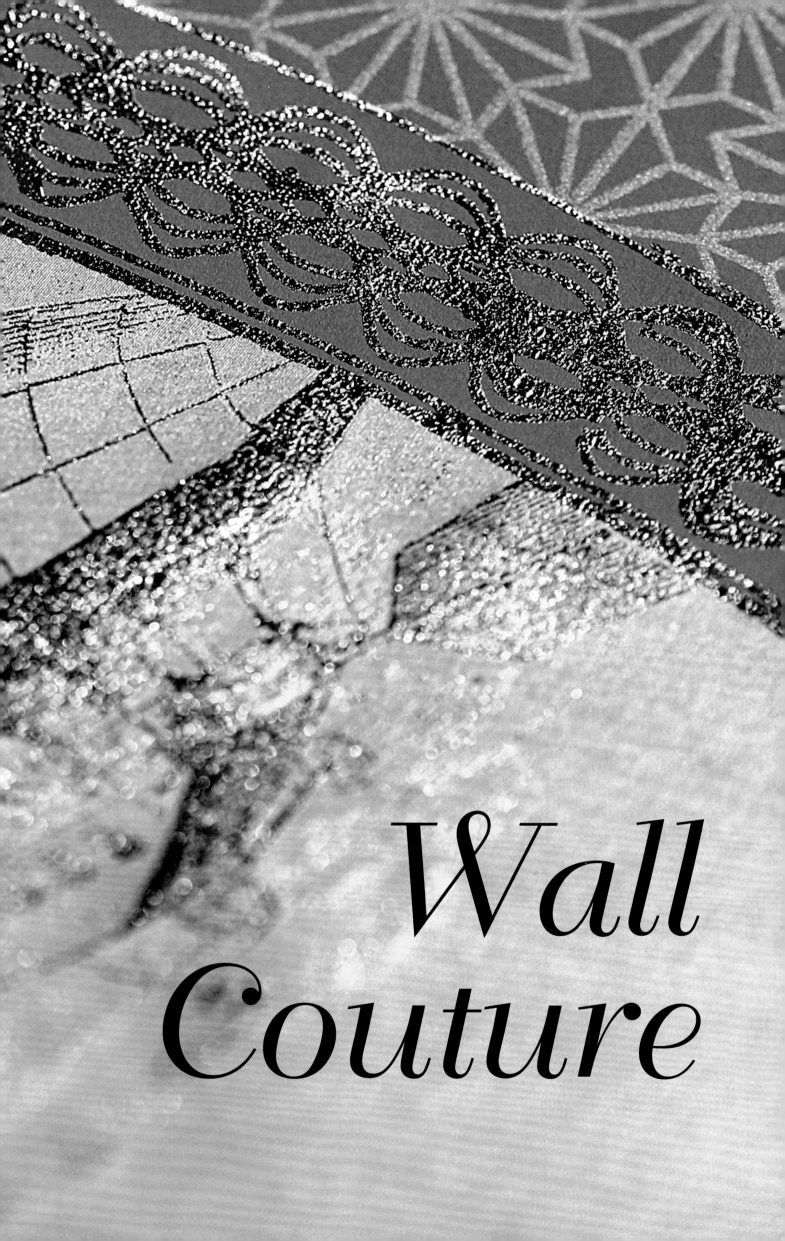

Wall
Couture

Digital innovations mean nothing to the creative minds in this chapter. These are the couturiers of wallpaper, who think only in terms of natural pigments, traditional glues and the feel of the finished product.

Some of them claim an affiliation with the great designers of the 18th century, while others remain fiercely contemporary, but all of them believe in the fundamentals of physical involvement and handcrafted techniques. And most importantly, they understand the extraordinary pleasure of engaging with wallpaper in an intimate way. Like magicians or alchemists, they immerse themselves in their materials, revelling in colour and texture. In their expert hands, luxury and originality take on a new meaning. Are they artists or artisans? That is the question.

Living traditions

Keeping the history of Zuber alive

The French firm Zuber & Cie has weathered two world wars and several economic crises, and remains the only wallpaper firm to have survived for two hundred years. The company experienced a downturn in its fortunes following the Second World War, continuing to rely heavily on manual production at a time of frenzied industrial growth, and did not bounce back until the 1970s, and only then for a brief period. It was the heiress to a firm of paper merchants in Nice who bravely – some might say recklessly – took over the reins in 1984. Woken from its dormant state, Zuber returned to its first loves – handmade wallpapers and panoramas – and since then the firm has devoted itself to bespoke manufacture, prioritizing luxury and exclusivity and relying on the techniques developed by Jean Zuber and his descendants. The idea was to perpetuate his work and also to invent new products adapted to suit contemporary tastes. No new motifs are designed, since the skilled engravers have long since passed away. Instead, the firm exploits the extraordinary collection of antique woodblocks (a hundred and fifty thousand in total) that are still stored in tottering piles in the factory basement. It is from this treasure trove that today's designers unearth old designs and restore them to life by using new colourways, materials or techniques.

Above and opposite: *Blockprinting in the Zuber workshop. Skills such as these have been passed down through generations and require a great deal of concentration and precision.*

Trade secrets

At the Zuber headquarters in Rixheim, watched over by the ghost of their founder, the printers still work on massive oak tables, practising their time-honoured craft. Nothing has changed. The place looks as it always did; the tools are the same, and the printers' hand movements are the same — small, smooth and precise, honed by long years of apprenticeship. Their wrists are supple, their eyes sharply focused. And the silence is profound, the atmosphere one of intense concentration. It almost feels like a monastery, far removed from the everyday world.

Up under the eaves of this listed building is the workshop where the panoramas are produced, as slowly and painstakingly as an illuminated manuscript. Commissions keep coming, from top interior designers working for Russian oligarchs or luxury hotels. Reproducing the classic panoramas — 'Hindustan' (pages 52–53), 'Views of Brazil', 'Views of North America', 'Eldorado' (page 51), 'Isola Bella', 'Japanese Garden' (pages 48–49) — is a major undertaking, quite staggering in its complexity. It is normal to use as many as 1,500 individual woodblocks — which took some twenty engravers more than a year to make — and up to 250 colours for each of the thirty panoramas designed in the 19th century, all of which have enchanted many generations of onlookers.

Inch by inch, colour by colour, the printers advance slowly, manoeuvring their blocks with loving care. The colours specified by the original 'mixers' are precisely formulated and the tempo of the work is painstakingly slow; but the eye is the ultimate judge. While tiny irregularities are guarantees of authenticity, even a single error means that the whole thing has to be scrapped — and a fortune goes down the drain.

The printers use distemper paints for their thick texture that gives life and a flexible finish to the motif. Zuber skies have a magical beauty, their colours graduated according to a system developed in house; the job can be more like choreographing a ballet than painting a picture. These craftspeople are sorcerers' apprentices and true national treasures.

A taste for nostalgia

The skilful fingers of François-Xavier Richard

Ten years ago, after falling in love with antique wallpaper designs, François-Xavier Richard, a former art teacher, embarked on a mission to revive traditional blockprinting techniques, while developing his own personal methods in tandem with the old ones. At his workshop, the Atelier d'Offard, Richard brings beautiful old motifs to life, printing them by hand in the grand tradition, but also using computer graphics when he needs to produce an engraving or fine tune a design, thereby wiping out with a click of the mouse the frontiers between the major manufacturers of the 18th century and his own little sanctuary in Joué-les-Tours. He is a time traveller, bent over his printing tables, dancing back and forth between his pots of glue and his pigments, amid boxes stuffed with designs and drawers overflowing with samples. The Atelier d'Offard straddles two worlds: it is a workshop not unlike those found in 19th-century Paris, with their pungent smell of animal glue, but at the same time it is a laboratory equipped with more contemporary tools, built up over time with his father's help as the commissions flowed in.

It is this synthesis that allows Richard and his staff to tackle the monumental task of reproducing and reinventing a range of wallpapers – including embossed, gilded and flocked designs – that once earned a fortune for the great manufacturers of the golden age. Richard takes great pleasure in recreating an old design from fragments, rather like an archaeologist at work; but he also collaborates on projects with contemporary firms such as Jacques Garcia, Jacques Grange, Alberto Pinto and David Hicks, savouring the opportunity to break new creative ground.

Left and opposite: *Just a few of the treasures at the Atelier d'Offard.*

Aware of his keen focus on quality, his clients sometimes send him paper fragments from the other side of the world, and Richard uses these to bring an original design back to life. He also creates authentic reproductions for museums, palaces and private houses, including an Art Nouveau house in Brussels, the Palacio Ajuda in Lisbon, the châteaux of Fontainebleau and Malmaison in France, and Biltmore House, the former Vanderbilt family mansion in Asheville, North Carolina. In the course of this work, Richard has acquired the rights to four designs by Jacques-Émile Ruhlmann and has now opened an online catalogue offering a range of original designs to the general public – who are also welcomed into his Ali Baba's cave one day a month. The catalogue emerged from various projects focusing on new motifs and now offers a rich and eclectic mix of damasks, arabesques and imitation drapery, together with geometrics. All in all, it is not hard to see why this virtuoso was awarded the prestigious Liliane Bettencourt Prize in 2009.

In search of authenticity

Chris Ohrstrom and Steve Larson are the American ambassadors for historical wallpaper. Adelphi Paper Hangings, their Virginia-based company, is housed in an exact replica of an 18th-century workshop, complete with hand presses, and is the only wallpaper firm in the US to commercially blockprint historic papers. Ohrstrom and Larson have gone to great lengths to get their colours just right, basing them on formulae from the 1765 book A Handmaiden to the Arts *by Robert Dossie. They work with distemper paints and engrave their own pearwood printing blocks, which they store in a stone cellar in the traditional manner. They utilize cotton fibre paper that replicates the texture and weight of the historical product and also use seamed rolls — made up of sheets glued end to end by hand — in order to recreate the slight horizontal ridges that are typical of pre-1850s wallpapers. As well as possessing an extensive collection of original designs dating from 1750 to 1930, ready to be reproduced, Adelphi also work with designs taken from the archives of institutions such as the Colonial Williamsburg Foundation and the Smithsonian Institution.*

Based in Massachusetts, John Buscemi has been working since 1986 with museums, collectors, historic houses, decorators and designers. His firm Belfry Historic Consultants now sources and supplies designs by some of the best craftspeople in the world, including David Skinner and Sons (Ireland), Hamilton Weston (UK), Atelier d'Offard and Lutson Goudleder (France), Duro and Lim & Handtryck (Sweden), and even imports from as far afield as Latvia.

Meanwhile, in the UK, designer Allyson McDermott also produces some splendid restorations and reproductions of historical wallpapers. With thirty years of experience behind her, McDermott is an expert in traditional embossing and blockprinting as well as being a specialist in Chinese wallpaper.

'Spiral Willow'
(c. 1920), a wallpaper
design by René
Crevel, now recreated
by Adelphi Paper
Hangings.

Adding a personal touch

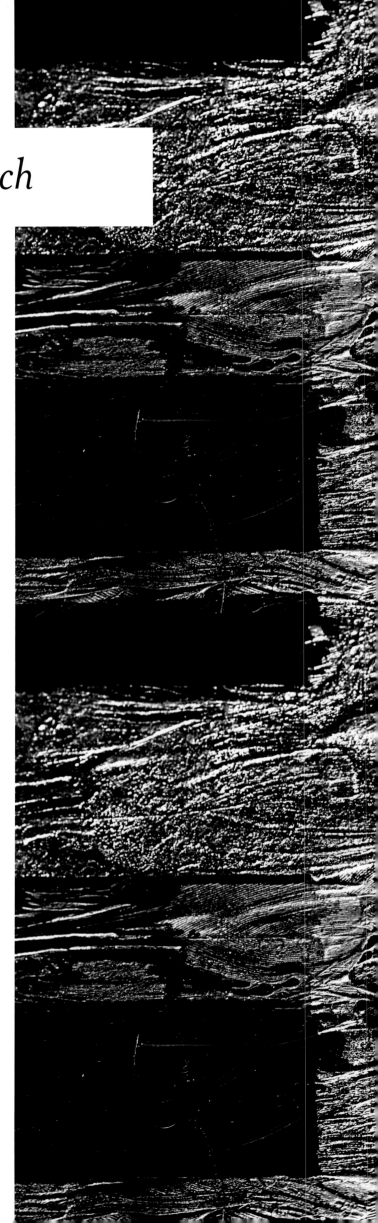

Anne Gelbard

Tulle, lace and organza vie for space with painted panels in Anne Gelbard's workshop. Dior, Balenciaga and Valentino are all fans of Gelbard's fabrics and leathers worked with copper, silver and gold leaf, and regularly commission new fabric designs from her for their collections. Gelbard's unique creations are so beautiful that they cause waves in the world of fashion, but as it happens, the artist would be hard pressed to choose between working with textiles and paper. Couture clothes, however gorgeous, are here today and gone tomorrow, and Gelbard wanted to work with something less ephemeral, to create objects that would form a backdrop to people's everyday lives. So she began designing wallpaper and now alternates between the two media, experimenting with both materials in a creative two-way process.

In her wallpaper designs (see right), diaphanous metallic leaf, a whole range of pigments and sparkling fairytale embroidery – elements fit for supermodels and movie stars – metamorphose walls into shimmering expanses, by means of a painstaking process of dyeing and screenprinting. Iridescent inks and unusual combinations – such as gold leaf and feathers – transform wallpaper into a series of precious panels of an ethereal beauty – just as a couture accessory can transform an outfit. 'Home couture' is how Gelbard describes her range. Interior designers are snapping it up and La Belle Juliette, a boutique hotel in Paris, has been decorated throughout in Gelbard wallpaper, as an added enticement to guests.

Florence Rolle-Desmarest

Abandoning a career as a financial consultant without a backward glance, Florence Rolle-Desmarest has dedicated her life to her abiding passion, the graphic arts. She operates primarily through her website, Intérieurs & Dépendance, selling home and garden furnishings and *objets d'art*, one-off pieces showcased in a rustic setting in the Île de France region. It was this traditional retreat that gave the designer inspiration for her first two gorgeous and very personal wallpaper designs, 'Le Boudoir Poudré' and 'Les Baroques'. The first of these is decorated with statue-like heads enlivened

with touches of gold and silver (see left), inspired by a stone mask that adorns the façade of her house. The second is an embossed wallpapers in imitation leather. These wallpapers are blockprinted on a hand-brushed or waxed base.

Rolle-Desmarest loves colour and has created an exquisite palette of pink, lavender, grey and pale green, with a light, powdery finish that gives her wallpapers a soft romantic look but also a certain robustness: this is the world of Sofia Coppola's *Marie Antoinette*, full of pastel shades with a contemporary twist. The designer is currently compiling an anthology of vintage wallpapers for collectors, and it will no doubt provide a rich source of inspiration for future designs.

Previous pages: *Anne Gelbard at work in her studio and two examples of the magical effects that couture wallpaper can create.*
Opposite: *'Le Boudoir Poudré' by Florence Rolle-Desmarest, available from Intérieurs & Dépendance.*
Below: *'Herbes Folles' by Agnès Emery.*
Overleaf, from left to right: *'Chinoiseries' by Anne Gelbard, 'Mangrove' by Dominos, 'Peliculea 3D ' by Maud Vantours, and 'Tree' by Ulgad'Or.*

Deborah Bowness

Deborah Bowness is already a star in the world of wallpaper. Philippe Starck and Paul Smith have embraced her designs and Christian Lacroix used them to decorate the walls of his Hôtel du Petit Moulin in Paris. Bowness began making wallpaper seven years ago, using digital graphics that are reworked by hand, allowing her imagination completely free reign. She was one of the first designers to create single hand-finished paper drops. The dresses in faded colours casually dangling from hangers and the retro standard lamps with their shades askew are just two designs by this queen of the trompe l'oeil and have become worldwide bestsellers. Unashamedly combining traditional techniques and digital technology, she creates a relaxed and familiar world where the simplest of subjects can be transformed through her unusual interpretation. Every design is slightly offbeat, whether it depicts a chaotic and overloaded bookcase, a precarious pile of vintage storage boxes, a solitary chair against the wall, or the classical damask pattern above a fake wooden dado in the Illusions of Grandeur series. 'Don't take us too seriously', these wallpapers seem to say, and they are adaptable designs that fit comfortably into any environment. Bowness designs a world that is unconventional, bold and poetic: a true graphic success story.

Ulgad'Or

Gabor Ulveczki has always wanted to give his
materials a life of their own. He chiefly works
with metal leaf and the gilded wallpapers created
in his Ulgad'Or atelier are worthy of a jeweler.
Ulveczki has devised a unique process – involving
the oxidation and corrosion of thin sheets of gold,
copper, silver and aluminium – that produces
unusual colour effects and a stunning play of
light and shade. His spectacular baroque and
contemporary wallpaper designs (see right) can
turn any room into a dazzling stage set. Because
of the delicate nature of the work and the valuable
materials used, the atelier also works in the age-
old domino format, making every piece a glittering
miniature work of art.

Ulveczki is always looking for new ideas and has
also designed a collection on Japanese wallpapers,
made on the island of Shikoku. He is something of
an impresario and likes receiving clients in his Paris
showroom, where his transformative skills create
works with a spectacular sense of theatre.

Agnès Emery

Belgian architect and designer Agnès Emery has
taken her experiences – journeys, encounters,
objects and places she has fallen in love with – and
turned them into an unusual range of textiles,
paints, furnishings, tableware and wallpaper
designs (pages 207 and 212). She admits that she
took her time to embrace wallpaper: 'For a long
time, wallpaper was something that had to be
removed urgently to take possession of a place, an
essential return to the material of the wall before
any space could be taken over. In other words, I
perceived wallpaper as an enemy to be destroyed.
At the same time, I took a certain pleasure in the
slow job of stripping the paper, which revealed
successive layers whose increasingly old-fashioned
styles fascinated me. I even ended up keeping
some of the fragments, humble witnesses of a not
very long-gone past which perfectly recreated the
atmosphere of their time.'

These fragments and the memories that they
evoke have inspired Emery to come up with motifs
for a selection of subtly patterned wallpapers, some
handmade, some bespoke, some sold in rolls and
some in domino-style panel format. The panels
are manufactured in India using traditional craft
techniques, and she positions them carefully,
deliberately emphasizing the seams, as her own
way of adding a touch of modernity.

Above: *This Gabor Ulveczki
design for Ulgad'Or
features the baroque glitter
of metallic leaf paper.*
Opposite: *Two typically
offbeat designs by Deborah
Bowness.*

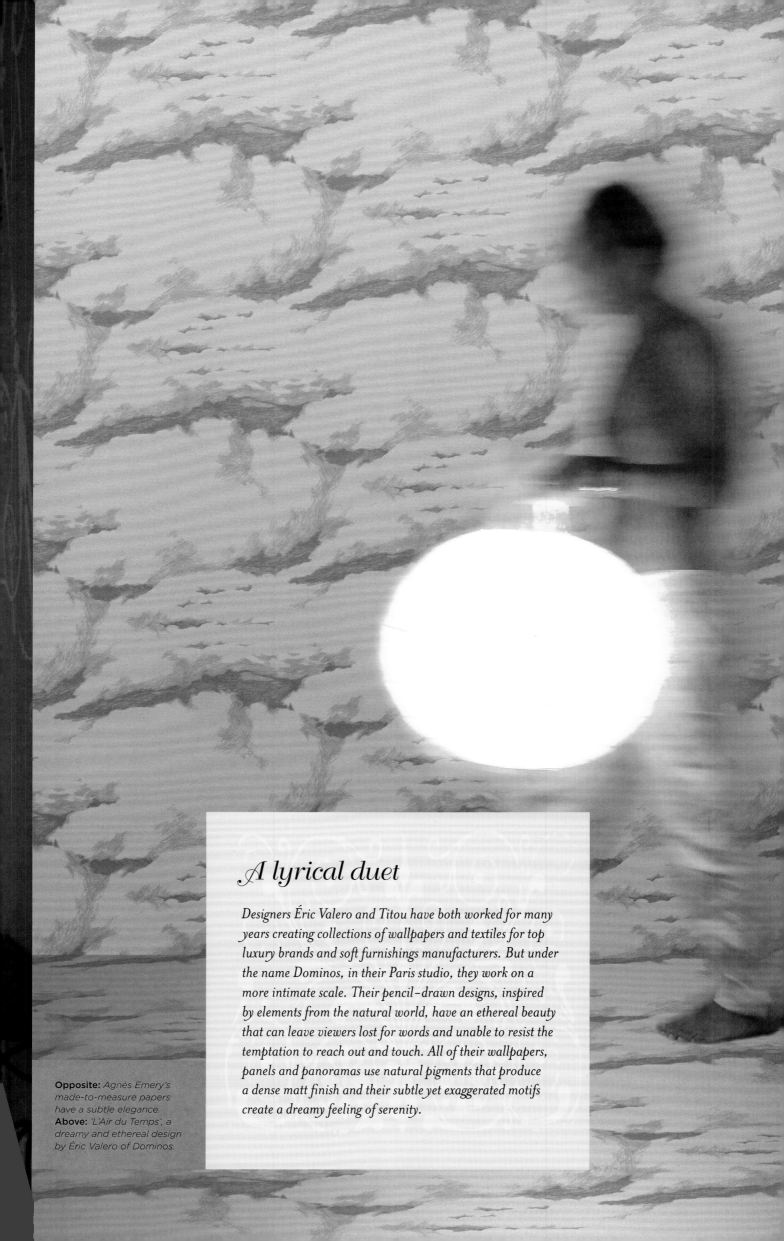

A lyrical duet

Designers Éric Valero and Titou have both worked for many years creating collections of wallpapers and textiles for top luxury brands and soft furnishings manufacturers. But under the name Dominos, in their Paris studio, they work on a more intimate scale. Their pencil-drawn designs, inspired by elements from the natural world, have an ethereal beauty that can leave viewers lost for words and unable to resist the temptation to reach out and touch. All of their wallpapers, panels and panoramas use natural pigments that produce a dense matt finish and their subtle yet exaggerated motifs create a dreamy feeling of serenity.

Opposite: *Agnès Emery's made-to-measure papers have a subtle elegance.*
Above: *'L'Air du Temps', a dreamy and ethereal design by Éric Valero of Dominos.*

Cabinets of curiosities

Despite today's high-speed world, some designers choose to celebrate a slower pace of living. They belong to the fields of fashion, photography and the fine arts, but regard the idea of being limited by a single medium as absurd in this modern day and age. Switching easily between disciplines, they nonetheless retain a distinct identity of their own. Rather than thinking of repetition and uniformity, they treat wallpaper like carbon paper, imprinting the world of their imagination onto its sensitive surface. Curious or kitsch, witty or warm, or simply full of nostalgia, their wallpapers are evocative works of art in themselves, sweeping us away to distant shores.

Vincent Darré's surreal elegance
Since Vincent Darré graduated from the famous Studio Berçot fashion school, he has worked with Yves Saint Laurent, Karl Lagerfeld and Andrée Putman, as a stylist for *Vogue* and as a stage costume designer. Darré is one of those multi-talented artists who cross boundaries with consummate ease.

Maison Darré, based in Paris's fashionable Rue du Mont-Thabor, reflects the unconventional spirit of its founder. Neither a gallery, nor a shop, nor a showroom, this space is what Darré himself describes as a 'research laboratory', a place where visitors find a whole series of intriguing and highly personal products, brought together with a Surrealist instinct for the strange and the fanciful.

The wallpaper collection – designed and produced by Darré himself – is anything but run-of-the-mill. Taking his inspiration from a 1950s book of botanical and anatomical illustrations, Darré produced two variant designs, one showing plants, the other insects (see opposite). But in this sanctum where uniqueness is the ultimate virtue, the repeat motifs used on conventional wallpaper would have been unthinkable. Darré's wallpaper is therefore sold in huge panels, almost panoramic in size, each featuring a single image. Dramatic in white on black, or more restrained in black on white, these designs are strange and striking but also extremely elegant, conferring a daring note of sophistication and eccentricity on any interior.

Aurélie Mathigot's threads of history
Aurélie Mathigot is one of those artists for whom wallpaper forms part of a global approach to design, one element within a spectrum of creative pursuits. Mathigot has worked in many media and uses various textile techniques including embroidery, crochet and knitting, in each case brilliantly reinventing them. Most of her works involve some kind of *trompe l'oeil* effect, a switch of proportions, or a means of changing the context of a motif so that it takes on a different meaning. She uses a wealth of materials, but in such a way that it is hard to recognize them for what they are.

For her wallpaper designs, she tends to unearth old designs and allows her imagination to play with the possibilities that they suggest, before meticulously reworking them. Her task, as she sees it, is to give physical existence to the things we know in our minds but cannot always perceive with our eyes, to bring them to life. She creates this reality through texture and touch, through her use of materials and her skills as a craftswoman. In her decorative panel papers for The Collection (page 193), a photograph of an ornate chair, decorated with real sequins, stands in front of a wall made up of other images: a white dress, a heap of folded fabrics or scattered postcards. All are highlighted with embroidery stitches – the Mathigot trademark.

Acting creatively

In line with its policy of collaborating with artist friends, Maison Darré is producing a wallpaper designed by French actress, singer and scriptwriter Valérie Lemercier — who also has a talent, it seems, for drawing. 'Drawing is a bit like the stage,' she says. 'You can do all sorts of things with a blank piece of paper. On stage, you can move from one world to another in two seconds, and you can take people with you — you don't need any props. The only difference is that with drawing you're more home bound. And that's what I dream of, in a way: to stay at home for ever and never go out again!' Safely surrounded by her own wallpaper, of course.

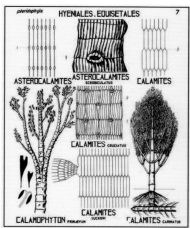
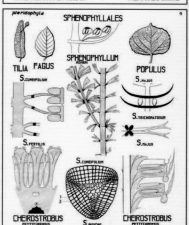
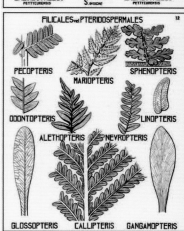
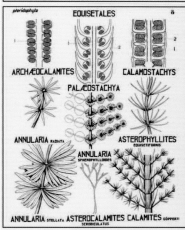
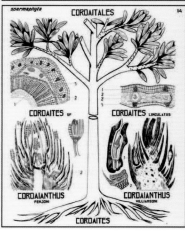
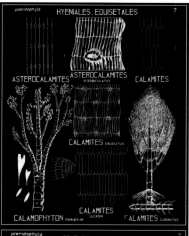
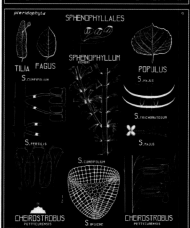
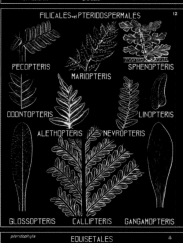
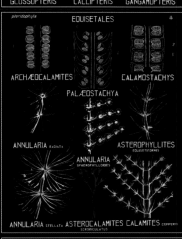
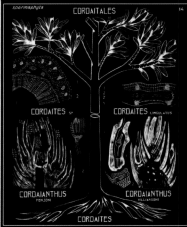

Above: 'Métamorph'os' by Vincent Darré. This bold and eccentric design imitates plates from a natural history book.
Overleaf: A black and white trompe l'oeil design by Maison Martin Margiela adorns a suite at Les Sources de Caudalie, a hotel near Bordeaux.

Putting paper in the picture

Catherine Ledner, a photographer based in Los Angeles, is best known for her charming and witty animal portraits, which can be seen on her website Catherine's Animals *and in her book* Animal House. *As a backdrop for these images, she chooses vivid retro wallpapers, turning the series into a sort of surreal catalogue of American design from the fifties with a zoological twist.*

Opposite, background: *A kaleidoscopic design by Catherine Cocherel.* **Opposite, inset:** *One of a range of digitally manipulated motifs by Rachel de Joode.*

The result is a strangely charming and painterly creation, a flat image with a three-dimensional feel. It could almost be described as a vertical sculpture, gentle yet bold at the same time. These wallpapers are a charming outlet for Mathigot's reflections on the passage of time.

Rachel de Joode's body art

Dutch artist and photographer Rachel de Joode has adopted a similar aesthetic but a different approach in her wallpaper collection for Soonsalon (opposite). Taking her inspiration from everyday life, she has developed a series of designs based around her own photographs and the classic wallpaper principle of repetition. At first glance, what we see is an apparently innocent geometric design, but closer inspection reveals that the shapes are made up of endlessly repeating female figures – often scantily clad – that form a kind of human kaleidoscope with a strong fashion aesthetic.

De Joode's approach to wall decoration is both surreal and sensual, and she uses a delicious palette of tempting colours that are reflected in the names of designs such as 'Sweetpepper', 'HoneyPie', 'Angelcake' and 'Triplefrosted'.

Martin Margiela's illusions

One of fashion's most private designers, Belgian-born Martin Margiela, has also invited the public to explore his creative world via a different route – wallpaper. At the request of his clients, who love the decor of his stores, Margiela transposed his pared-down aesthetic to wallpaper via a new interpretation of panoramic papers. He came up with self-adhesive paper in three motifs, all strongly inspired by the brand identity of his deconstructionist label.

His colours are neutral: shades of white, black and grey – the palette that is usually associated with Margiela. His first limited-edition wallpaper features *trompe l'oeil* doors, adapted from photographs of his former Paris headquarters in the Boulevard Poissonnière, the three motifs representing, respectively, a set of baroque-inspired double doors, a single door and an open doorway with a decorative moulding. The effect is particularly striking because the perspectives are designed to match the real location, giving these apparently innocent motifs a splendidly theatrical impact – not unlike their creator, Margiela, fashion's invisible but omnipresent designer. The wallpaper was produced at the end of 2009, just as Margiela was leaving his Paris base, pulling the door closed behind him – a fact that makes these subtle and curious motifs all the more engaging.

Catherine Cocherel's performances on paper

The approach taken by artist Catherine Cocherel starts with a live performance, which is then captured in an image on a wall. For more than ten years, Cocherel has worked in fields including land art, body art, installations and graphic design. She explores the relationship between the natural and human worlds, creating whole new realms – human, organic, plant – in which gauze, soil and seeds are woven or twisted into vines that imprison her subjects. In the performance pieces entitled *Corps étrangers* (*Foreign Bodies*), the vines are sculpted around a piece of architecture or another space, or woven around the body of a dancer, whose movements are mirrored by the motions of these organic restraints. Each performance is site-specific and explores the concepts of interaction and confrontation.

It is this weaving together of ephemeral organic components that Cocherel has chosen to transpose onto wallpaper, as a kind of testimony to the living moment. Each performance is photographed and filmed and these images are digitally manipulated to create a graphic design, in which the artist reworks the lines, shapes and colours and adjusts the scale to create a *mise en abyme* effect (see opposite). The result is a series of photographic self-portraits that

Designs by Maud
Vantours, in whose
hands wallpaper
can become an
installation of bold
or delicate layers.

take us on a journey of the imagination through the worlds of pop art, embroidery, weaving, fractal mathematics and kaleidoscopes.

Seen from a distance, these motifs look like traditional wallpaper designs, but in close-up, the viewer's relationship with the design changes and the secrets of its composition are revealed. A magnifying glass, obligingly supplied by the artist, enables the viewer to engage playfully with the image, providing more intimate access to the details of form, colour and texture. Cocherel's body of work raises questions about life itself, and about the boundaries between nature and artifice.

Maud Vantours's layers of discovery

Maud Vantours was just a recent graduate from the École Duperré, a renowned French school of design, when she began to make a name for herself with her free interpretations of the theme of wallpaper. Her works are mainly in the form of decorative panels, made of sheets of paper stuck together and trimmed by hand, or arranged into overlapping transparent layers with cut-out shapes, so that the motifs break up, forming an endless series of superimposed shadows and relief effects. Juggling bold colours – inspired by the walls of colonial houses in Cuba – and light and shade, Vantours creates wallcoverings that are more like installations, engaging in a two-way relationship with the wall and embedding it with a sense of movement. The plant world is a major source of inspiration for this young artist, whose wall art (see left) enchants the eye and explores the concept of time and its layers.

The future's bright

Art by the roll

Digital art galleries are a flourishing online phenomenon. Blandine Morel and David Poissenot set up theirs – exclusively dedicated to wallpaper – in 2006. The rationale behind Wallpapers by Artists was twofold: to offer customers a series of original designs and to offer artists a new medium of expression. They already have twenty designs in their catalogue, each by an established artist and all designed to be different.

The project began with the Swiss artist Olivier Mosset, a close associate of French minimalist Daniel Buren; Mosset's yellow monochrome wallpaper was hugely popular with collectors. He was followed by Marc Camille Chaimowicz and his *toile de Jouy* pastiche decorated with quirky little cherubs, Geoffroy Gross and his blood-spattered stripes, and Loïc Raguénès, with his curious dachshunds (see left). Since then, other contemporary artists have added their names to the gallery, attracted by the opportunity of working in a different way and on an unusual sort of 'canvas'. These works may come in the format of a standard roll of wallpaper, but they are printed in distemper colour using traditional machines to give the beautiful matt texture and look of a real painting.

Art lovers like the idea of pasting up a wallpaper that is an imaginative world in its own right, with a subtext that is often waiting to be deciphered. Francis Baudevin's broad stripes in turquoise and sky blue, also for Wallpapers by Artists, are a tribute to the *Tintin* books, whose colours they replicate.

Samuel Rousseau's moving motifs

Samuel Rousseau is a Swiss multimedia artist who works predominantly in the field of video. His beautiful and sensitive video projections include a 'video wallpaper' (created in 2003), which the artist himself installs in a client's home, adjusting it on site to fit the dimensions of the wall. Clients can choose any three from a set of twenty-five limited-edition designs, which include a 1950s-style floral motif, flying saucers, little cars and a kaleidoscope of giant numerals. These dreamlike images are not static: a remote control system means that the design can be switched from one motif to another, or turned off altogether when what the customer wants is a bare wall.

Thinking differently

'Constantly curious' could be the motto of Larry Allam and Morgan Vo Dinh. This duo, who are in their thirties and both passionate about interior design, as well as being quite unable to resist a joke, started out by opening the boutique Think & More in the Rue Saint-Honoré in Paris. It began a temple to paper in all its forms — wallpaper, books, photographs — but has recently expanded to include a selection of designer objects and works by contemporary artists. The store regularly showcases designs by Jean-Charles de Castelbajac, creator of a bold wallpaper range (pages 70–71, 112–113), and stunning creations by Munchausen (pages 154–155). Its spectacular wallpapers are selected with great care and include designs by Timorous Beasties (pages 224, 237), Tom Dixon, Piero Fornasetti, Louise Body (page 191), Miss Print, Marimekko and Tres Tintas, and the store has recently launched its own collection of digital designs by Catherine Cocherel. Always on the look out for new innovations, the Think & More team are continuing to explore the evolving world of wallpaper and follow every development with an expert eye.

Conclusion

In the end, wallpaper is only paper – a fragile, ephemeral, ordinary material.
And yet, when combined with imagination and ingenuity, it has proved itself to
be an extraordinarily creative medium, a form of decoration that bridges the spaces
between art, craftsmanship and industry. Its changing textures, colours and motifs
have not been chance developments; even before the advent of modern design studios,
wallpaper was already foreshadowing social change, embracing new technology and
anticipating fashion. At one time it seemed to fade out of the picture, but wallpaper
remained as a discreet but inextricable element of our daily lives.

In the hands of contemporary designers, however, it has revived and reclaimed
its former glories. Once used to line an entire room, it can now be found adorning
a bold statement wall, climbing the ceiling, unfurling horizontally across a room or
reduced to a single stunning drop, like a work of art in its own right. As technology
advances, it can become magnetic, digital and interactive, setting its own rules and
becoming so much more than a negligible backdrop. Nor is wallpaper confined to
the intimacy of our homes; it can now be a scenesetter in any environment, creating
an atmosphere or subtly reinforcing a brand message.

In the hands of a few aficionados, passionate about beauty in all its forms,
wallpaper has managed to hold on to its traditional roots and has even found its way
into museums and art galleries. We may fall in and out of love with wallpaper as the
decades roll by, but somehow the affair never truly ends.

*'Butterfly' from the
Entomology collection
by Timorous Beasties.*

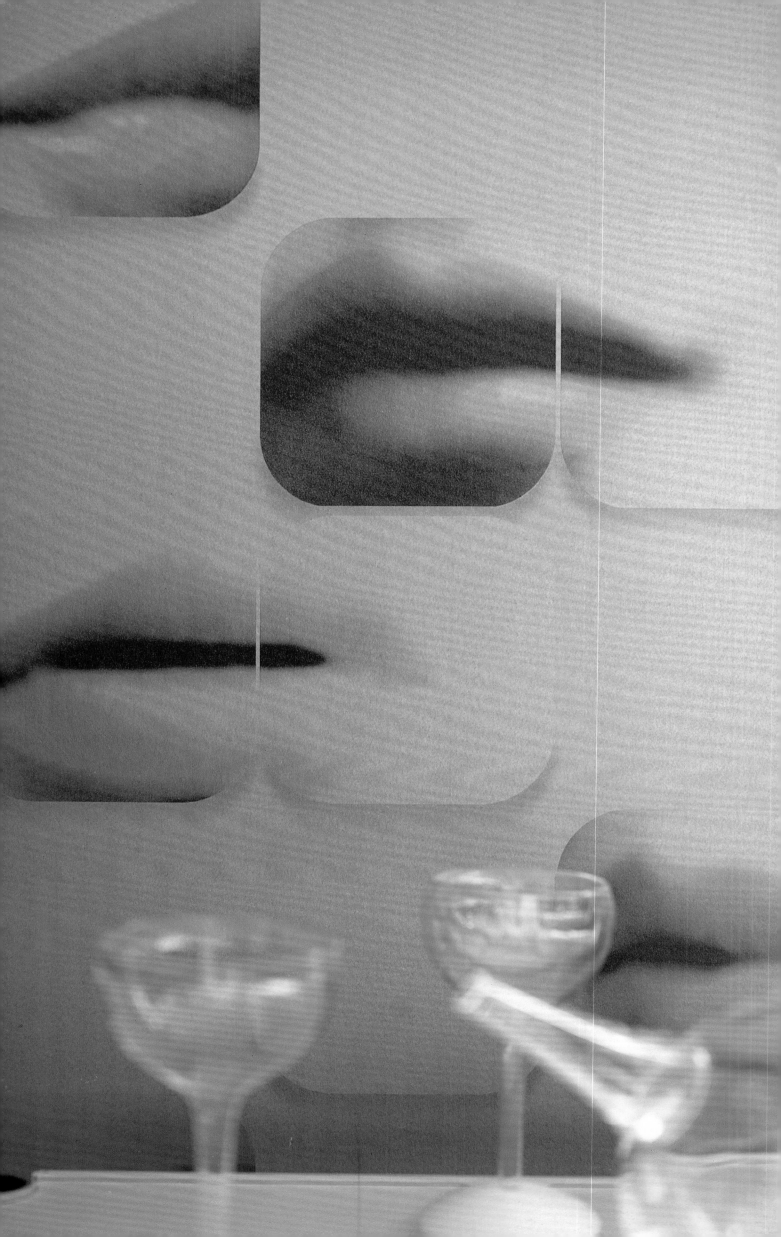

'Lipstick', a limited edition by Élitis.

Wallpaper collections worldwide

AUSTRALIA

Art Gallery of New South Wales
Sydney
www.artgallery.nsw.gov.au

National Gallery of Australia
Canberra
www.nga.gov.au

FRANCE

Musée des Arts Décoratifs
Palais du Louvre
Paris
Tel.: +33 (0)1 44 55 57 50
www.lesartsdecoratifs.fr

Bibliothèque Forney
Paris
Tel.: +33 (0)1 42 78 14 60

Musée du Papier Peint
Rixheim
Tel.: +33 (0)3 89 64 24 56
www.museepapierpeint.org

**Centre de Documentation
Joseph Dufour**
Tramayes
Tel.: +33 (0)3 85 50 57 04
www.dufour.ot-tramayes.com

**Musée Départemental Maurice
Denis Le Prieuré**
Saint-Germain-en-Laye
Tel.: +33 (0)1 39 73 77 87

GERMANY

Deutsches Tapetenmuseum
Kassel (closed for renovation
until 2013)
www.museum-kassel.de

SWEDEN

Nordiska Museet
Stockholm
www.nordiskamuseet.se

SWITZERLAND

Musée du Papier Peint
Mézières
Tél.: + 41 26 652 06 90
www.museepapierpeint.ch

UNITED KINGDOM

The Geffrye Museum of the Home
London
www.geffrye-museum.org.uk

**Museum of Domestic Design
& Architecture**
Middlesex University
www.moda.mdx.ac.uk

Ulster Museum
Belfast
www.nmni.com/um

Victoria & Albert Museum
London
www.vam.ac.uk

The Whitworth Art Gallery
Manchester
www.whitworth.manchester.ac.uk

UNITED STATES

**Cooper-Hewitt National
Design Museum**
New York
www.cooperhewitt.org

Fine Arts Museum
San Francisco
www.famsf.org

Glen Burnie Museum
Winchester, VA
www.shenandoahmuseum.org

**Museum of Art, Rhode Island
School of Design**
Providence, RI
www.risdmuseum.org

Museum of Fine Arts
St Petersburg, FL
www.fine-arts.org

Philadelphia Museum of Arts
Philadelphia, PA
www.philamuseum.org

*'Exotic Dandy',
a limited edition
by Élitis.*

Useful addresses

Designers and stores

UNITED KINGDOM

Absolute Zero°
Tel.: +44 (0)20 7737 6767
www.absolutezerodegrees.co.uk

Johanna Basford
johannabasford.com

Beyond the Valley
Tel.: +44 (0)20 7437 7338
www. beyondthevalley.com

Louise Body
Tel.: +44(0)773 490 7357
www.louisebody.com

Deborah Bowness
Tel.: +44(0)1757 248 500
www.deborahbowness.com

Cole & Son
For international stockists, see:
www.cole-and-son.com

Colefax and Fowler
For international stockists, see:
www.colefax.com

Claire Coles Design
Tel.: +44(0)20 3214 3114
www.clairecolesdesign.co.uk

Custhom
Tel.: +44 (0)7843 241 413
www.custhom.co.uk

Designers Guild
For online store and international
stockists, see:
www.designersguild.com

Design Centre Chelsea Harbour
www.designcentrechelseaharbour.co.uk

Agnès Emery
c/o Retrouvius
Tel.: + 44 (0)208 969 0222
www.emeryetcie.com

Farrow & Ball
For online store and international
stockists, see:
www.farrow-ball.com

Anna French
Tel.: +44 (0)20 7737 6555
www.annafrench.co.uk

Fromental
Tel.: +44 (0)20 3410 2000
www.fromental.co.uk

Graham & Brown
Tel.: 0800 328 8452
www.grahambrown.com

Allegra Hicks
Tel.: +44 (0)20 7730 3275
www.allegrahicks.com

David Hicks
www.davidhicks.co.uk

Tracy Kendall Wallpaper
Tel.: +44 (0)20 7640 9071
www.tracykendall.com

Kuboaa by Andrew Hardiman
www.kuboaa.co.uk

The Little Greene Paint Company
Tel.: +44 (0)161 23 00 880
www.littlegreene.com

Allyson McDermott Historic Interiors
Tel.: +44 (0)1594 510003
www.allysonmcdermott.com

France's wallpaper museum

The Musée du Papier Peint, or Museum of Wallpaper, was opened in 1983 in Rixheim, France, a town with an historical tradition of wallpaper making and home to the Zuber company. The goals of the museum are to preserve and restore historical wallpapers, to act as an archive of contemporary designs and documents from the industry's past, and to make all of these things available to the public and to specialist historians.

A visit to the museum is a colourful journey through centuries of designs. Eleven panoramic papers are on permanent display; the museum also holds regular themed exhibitions that focus on different aspects of its collections. In addition, it houses a selection of the ingenious tools and equipment that have been used to print wallpaper both by hand and by machine, dating from the 17th century to the 1930s.

'Paradiso' by London studio Fromental.

Nono
Tel.: +44 (0)845 271 7333
www.nono.co.uk

Osborne & Little
For international stockists, see:
www.osborneandlittle.com

Sanderson
For international stockists, see:
www.sanderson-uk.com

Timorous Beasties
Tel.: +44 (0)141 337 2622
www.timorousbeasties.com

Emily Todhunter Collection
Tel.: +44 (0)20 7349 9935
www.todhunterearle.com

Erica Wakerly
Tel.: +44 (0)7940 577 620
www.ericawakerly.com

Jocelyn Warner
Tel.: +44 (0)20 7375 3754
jocelynwarner.com

Brian Yates
Tel.: +44 (0)1524 35035
www.brian-yates.co.uk

UNITED STATES

Adelphi Paper Hangings
Tel.: +1 518 284 9066
www.adelphipaperhangings.com

Art People Wallcovering Inc
Tel.: +1 212 431 4865

Anthropologie
For international stores, see:
www.anthropologie.com

Belfry Historic Consultants
www.belfryhistoric.com

Brett Design
brettdesigninc.com

Brunschwig et Fils
www.brunschwig.com

Cavern Home
www.cavernhome.com

Innovations in Wallcoverings
Tel.: +1 212 308 1179
www.innovationsusa.com

Makelike
makelike.com

Schumacher
Tel.: +1 212 415 3900
www.fschumacher.com

Walnut Wallpaper
Tel.: +1 323 932 9166
www.walnutwallpaper.com

Aimee Wilder
aimeewilder.com

AUSTRALIA

Ilias Fotopoulos
Tel.: +61 2 9664 3080
www.ilias.com.au

Scandinavian Wallpaper & Décor
Tel.: +61 (08) 9387 1549
www.wallpaperdecor.com.au

The Selvedge Group
Tel.: +61 1300 721 157
www.theselvedgegroup.com.au

Signature Prints
www.signatureprints.com.au

BELGIUM

Buzzispace
www.buzzispace.com

Hookedonwalls
www.hookedonwalls.com

Omexco
Tel.: +32 16 40 18 80
www.omexco.be

CANADA

Charles Rupert Designs
Historic wallpapers and fabrics
Tel.: +1 250 384 1892
www.charlesrupertdesigns.com

Rollout
Custom wallpaper studio
Toronto tel.: +1 416 960 0110
Vancouver tel.: +1 604 681 3780
www.rollout.ca

Umbra
Tel.: +1 800 387 5122
www.umbra.com

FINLAND

Marimekko
For international stockists, see:
www.marimekko.fi

FRANCE

5.5 Designers
Tel.: +33 (0)1 48 00 83 50
www.cinqcinqdesigners.com

Alyos Design
Murals on demand
Tel.: +33 (0)3 89 74 10 75
www.alyos.eu

Atelier d'Offard
Tel.: + 33 (0)2 47 67 93 22
www.atelierdoffard.com

Au Fil des Couleurs
Tel.: + 33 (0)1 45 44 74 00
www.aufildescouleurs.com

'Lipstick', a limited edition by Élitis.

Casamance and Camengo
For international stockists, see:
www.casamance.com

Co-Balt Productions
www.co-balt.com

The Collection
Tel.: + 33 (0)1 42 77 04 20
www.thecollection.fr

Dominos
dominosparis.blogspot.com

Élitis
Tel.: + 33 (0)1 45 51 51 00
www.elitis.fr

Pierre Frey
For international stockists of the Pierre Frey, Boussac and Braquenié brands, see:
www.pierrefrey.com

Anne Gelbard
Tel.: + 33 (0)1 43 14 60 10
www.annegelbard.com

Ich & Kar
www.ichetkar.fr

Iksel
Tel.: + 33 (0)1 42 96 51 97
www.iksel.com

In Création
Tel.: + 33 (0)6 08 82 53 47
www.increation.fr

Intérieurs & Dépendance
www.interieursetdependance.fr

Koziel
Tel.: +33 (0)3 20 58 83 06
www.koziel.fr

Lutèce
For wallpaper by Jean-Charles de Castelbajac and Zofia Rostad, see:
www.lutece-gpfb.com

Maison Vincent Darré
Tel.: + 33 (0)1 42 60 27 97
www.maisondarre.com

Moove-Paper
Moveable magnetic wallpaper
www.moovepaper.fr

MuZéo Collection
Artworks on demand
www.muzeocollection.com

Nobilis
Tel.: + 33 (0)1 43 29 21 50
www.nobilis.fr

Florence Rolle-Desmarest
Tel.: + 33 (0)1 47 05 05 05
www.interieursetdependance.fr

Saint Honoré Wallcoverings
Wallpapers by Munchausen
Tel.: + 33 (0)6 20 61 37 64
www.sainthonorewallcoverings.com

Think & More
Tel.: + 33 (0)1 40 26 18 51
www. thinkandmore.com

Ulgad'Or
Tel.: + 33 (0)1 42 71 05 77
www.ulgador.com

Maud Vantours
www.maudvantours.com

Wallpapers by Artists
www.wallpapersbyartists.com

Zuber
Tel.: + 33 (0)3 89 44 13 88
www.zuber.fr

GERMANY

Markus Benesch
www.markusbeneschcreates.com

Berlintapete: Wallpaper on Demand
www.berlintapete.de

Lars Contzen
www.contzentrade.com
www.lars-contzen.de

Dr Nice
www.drnice.net

Endless Wallpaper
Designs by Bettina Gerlach
Tel.: +49 (0)211 97 71 82 36
www.endless-wallpaper.de

GoHome Urban Wallpaper
Tel.: +49 (0)221 932 81 82
www.timetogohome.de

Marburg
www.marburg.com

P van b
Tel.: +49 (0) 30 44 35 61 05
www.pvanb.com

Rasch
Tel.: +49 (0) 54 61 81 10
www.rasch.de

Single-Tapete
Tel.: +49 (0) 61 31/ 22 30 37
www.single-tapete.de

Tapeten der 70er
Tel.: +49 36625 50556
wallpaperfromthe70s.com

IRELAND

Charles Newhaven Interior Designers
www.charlesnewhaven.ie

Ryan Wallcoverings
Tel.: + 353 (0)1 4640099
www.ryanwallcoverings.com

Collette Ward Interior Design & Decoration
Tel.: + 353 (0)402 36585
www.collettewardinteriors.ie

ITALY

Jannelli & Volpi
www.jannellievolpi.it

Montecolino
Tel.: +39 030 98 33 61
www.montecolino.it

Wall & Decò
Tel.: +39 0544 918012
www.wallanddeco.com

Zambaiti Parati
www.zambaitiparati.com

NETHERLANDS

Eijffinger
Tel.: +31 (0)79 3441200
www.eijffinger.com

The Frozen Fountain
Tel.: +31 (0)20 6229375
www.frozenfountain.nl

Maxalot Gallery
Tel.: +31 6 34346031
www.maxalot.com

Soonsalon
Tel.: +31 (0)224 54 32 70
www.soonsalon.com

Wannekes
Tel.: +31 (0) 6 21866026
www.wannekes.nl

NEW ZEALAND

The Inside
Tel.: +64 3 539 4469
www.theinside.co.nz

Netti & Gee
Tel.: +64 9 360 0214
www.nettiandgee.co.nz

PORTUGAL

For-Arte
Tel.: +351 253 690 385
www.for-arte.com

SOUTH AFRICA

The Silk and Cotton Co.
Tel.: +27 011 448 2578
www.silkco.co.za

SPAIN

Coordonné
Tel.: +34 915 760 963
www.coordonne.es

Ana Montiel
www.anamontiel.com

MC La esencia del Color
www.mc-pinturas.com

Tres Tintas
Tel.: +34 934 544 338
www.trestintas.com

Ybarra & Serret
Tel.: +34 915 102 062
www.ybarrayserret.com

SWEDEN

Bantie
Tel.: +46 8 666 9605
www.bantie.se

Decor Maison
Tel.: +46 33 125 400
www.decormaison.se

Sandberg
For international stockists, see:
www.sandbergab.se

Video wallpaper

Art-netart
Video wallpaper by Samuel Rousseau
www.art-netart.com

Galerie Anton-Weller
57, rue de Bretagne
75003 Paris
Tel.: 01 42 72 05 62
Email: antonweller@starnet.fr

Vintage wallpaper

E. W. Moore
39-43 Plashet Grove
London, E6 IAD
www.ewmoore.com

FunkyWalls
www.funkywalls.be

Secondhand Rose
230 5th Avenue, suite #510
New York, NY 10001
www.secondhandrose.com

'Kokeshi', a Japanese-inspired motif by Swedish design duo Bantie.

Further reading

Books

Alejandro Asensio, *Wallpaper*, Bath: Parragon Books, 2007

Timothy Brittain-Catlin, Jane Audas and Charles Stuckey, *The Cutting Edge of Wallpaper*, London: Black Dog Publishing, 2006

Joachim Fischer, *Tapeten, Papiers Peints, Wallpaper*, Cologne: Ullmann, 2008

Brenda Greysmith, *Wallpaper*, New York: Macmillan, 1976

Jan de Heer, *The Architectonic Colour: Polychromy in the Purist Architecture of Le Corbusier*, Rotterdam, 010 Publishers, 2010

Lesley Hoskins (ed.), *The Papered Wall: The History, Patterns and Techniques of Wallpaper*, London, Thames & Hudson, 2005

Joanne Kosuda-Warner, *Landscape Wallcoverings*, London: Scala; New York: Cooper-Hewitt National Design Museum, 2001

Terence Lane and Jessie Serle, *Australians at Home: A Documentary History of Australian Domestic Interiors from 1788 to 1914*, Melbourne: Oxford University Press, 1990

Catherine Lynn, *Wallpaper in America from the Seventeenth Century to World War I*, New York: W. W. Norton, 1980

Philippe Model, *Wallpaper: Decorative Art*, London: Scriptum, 2010

Odile Nouvel-Kammerer (ed.), *French Scenic Wallpaper: 1795–1865*, Paris: Flammarion, 2000

Marilyn Oliver Hapgood, *Wallpaper and the Artist: From Durer to Warhol*, New York: Abbeville, 1992

David Olivier, *Paint and Paper in Decoration*, New York: Rizzoli, 2007

Helen O'Neill, *Florence Broadhurst: Her Secret & Extraordinary Lives*, Melbourne: Hardie Grant, 2006

Mary Schoeser, *Sanderson: The Essence of English Decoration*, London: Thames & Hudson, 2010

Françoise Teynac, Pierre Nolot and Jean-Denis Vivien, *Wallpaper: A History*, London: Thames & Hudson, 1982

Carole Thibaud-Pomerantz, *Wallpaper: A History of Style and Trends*, Paris: Flammarion, 2009

Diane Waggoner, *The Beauty of Life: William Morris and the Art of Design*, London: Thames & Hudson, 2003

Exhibition catalogues

Home and Garden: Paintings and Drawings of English, Middle-Class Urban Domestic Spaces 1675-1914, London: Geffrye Museum, 2003

Kitsch to Corbusier: Wallpapers from the 1950s, New York: Cooper-Hewitt National Design Museum, Smithsonian Institution, 1995

A Popular Art: British Wallpapers 1930–1960, London: Silver Studio/Middlesex Polytechnic, 1990

Walls are Talking: Wallpaper, Art and Culture, Manchester: Whitworth Art Gallery, 2010

'Oriental Orchid' by Timorous Beasties.

Picture credits

Index